The Diabetic Chef

The Diabetic Chef

More Than 80 Simple but
Spectacular Recipes from One of
New York City's Top Chefs

Franklin Becker

BALLANTINE BOOKS

New York

A Ballantine Book
Published by The Random House Publishing Group

Copyright © 2005 by Franklin Becker

Published in the United States by Ballantine Books, an imprint of The Random House Publishing Group, a division of Random House, Inc., New York.

Ballantine and colophon are registered trademarks of Random House, Inc.

Library of Congress Cataloging-in-Publication Data is available upon request.

ISBN 0-345-47635-2

Printed in the United States of America

Ballantine Books website address: www.ballantinebooks.com

9 8 7 6 5 4 3 2 1

First Edition

Text design by Mary A. Wirth

Acknowledgments

This book is dedicated to the woman who has given me support, love, and understanding throughout the years, the woman who has given me a beautiful family, a wonderful home, and a reason to continue striving toward excellence: my wife, Jennifer. In addition, this book is dedicated to our two boys, Sean and Rory, who make our love complete.

Furthermore, I would like to thank those who have been there for me throughout the years. Thanks to my mom, dad, and brothers for testing my experiments early on in my career; my mother-in-law, Diane, for always providing my family with support; Grandma Peg; and Jo and Frank Quay (Nana and Grandpa), who have been there for us every step of the way.

I am also grateful to Anthony, because without you none of this would be happening now.

Professionally, I would like to thank the man who gave me the perfect launchpad for my career, David Napolitan.

Thanks to Fred Brightman, my longtime chef de cuisine at both Local and Capitale, whose talent behind the scenes is legendary.

Thanks to Arjuna Bull, Michael Jeanty, Moises Mena, and Chris D'amico, clearly some of the best cooks any chef could ask for—thanks to all of you.

Tony Fant, Neil Scott, and Brian Abel, thank you for your support. And thanks to Steven Hall and Sam Firer, the best publicists in the business.

Last but not least, thanks to Josh Greenwald and Suzanne Rostler for their tireless devotion to this book.

Contents

Foreword

On Nutrition

This is a book about food and how to have fun preparing it, savoring it, and sharing it with others. It is also about type 2 diabetes, a chronic disease in which your body no longer uses food the way it is supposed to.

At first, it may not seem worth the time and effort it takes to shop, prepare, and serve food for a diabetic diet. When many people are first diagnosed with diabetes, they believe that their relationship with food has been permanently changed for the worse. They think they can no longer enjoy their favorite meals or restaurants. Depressing visions of steamed spinach (without sauce), baked chicken (without skin), and bland Jell-O (without whipped cream) fill their heads.

If you have diabetes, you may have had similar thoughts. Perhaps your favorite foods are the ones that send your blood sugar soaring. Maybe you are confused about what to eat and simply assume that dining out or preparing exciting dishes at home is off-limits.

This chapter will show you how to have your cake and eat it too, but with some adjustments. If you don't believe me, try preparing the Steamed Bass with Shiitake Mushrooms and Baby Bok Choy (page 85), or the Warm Baked Apple with Golden Raisins and Walnuts (page 159); these and other recipes in this book will prove that eating well and satisfying your cravings are compatible with having type 2 diabetes. Although diabetes is bound to change your relationship with food in certain ways, it doesn't have to cramp your culinary style.

Diabetes can lead to changes in the way you think about food, which can have positive and lasting effects on your health, self-esteem, and quality of life. Diabetes is, for many people, a wake-up call to lose weight and get their culinary house in order. After being diagnosed with diabetes, you have the opportunity to improve your health significantly by following a more balanced eating plan. While some foods may have to be avoided, you can become more adventurous at the grocery store by adding new fruits, vegetables, and other healthy foods to your weekly shopping list.

You can also try new recipes, such as the ones in this book, that not only taste wonderful but also are healthy. In fact, most of the recipes in the following pages are low or moderate in fat and calories and packed with vitamins and minerals. Trying new recipes that require you to cook different foods or prepare the old standbys in new ways can both expand your culinary repertoire and improve your physical health. By adding new, healthier cooking techniques such as steaming, poaching, and sautéing, you might just learn to appreciate the way these techniques bring out the fresh and natural flavors of your food. These are all positive changes resulting from an adjustment in diet, and as a result you will feel better, look better, and have more energy than you did before.

The bottom line is that you can still visit your favorite restaurants, entertain your friends and family with wonderful meals at home, and enjoy the foods you have always loved, even after you have been diagnosed with type 2 diabetes. The trick is to arm yourself with a little nutrition knowledge that will help you balance your diet in a way that is sustainable for the long term.

The following pages will answer some of the questions you may have about food, nutrition, and diabetes. For example, what is a carbohydrate and how does it affect diabetes? What constitutes a balanced diet for diabetics? What types of foods should you limit or cut out altogether? Can you enjoy your usual glass of wine with dinner? Now let's get some answers.

What Is Diabetes?

First, let's start with the most basic question of all: what is diabetes? Type 2 diabetes is a chronic disease that affects an estimated 16 million to 18 million Americans. The onset of the disease is gradual; that is, it takes place over many years, and you may not be aware that you are headed for a diagnosis. What you might have noticed is that you were not feeling right for some time. You may have felt unusually tired, or your vision was getting blurry. Other symptoms include constantly feeling thirsty, along with urinating frequently. Or you might have had an infection or cut that would not heal. These are all signs and symptoms of type 2 diabetes.

Type 2 diabetes is defined as a disease in which your body does not respond to insulin. Insulin is a hormone, and hormones send signals to our cells telling them what to do and when to do it. Insulin is produced in a fist-size gland called the pancreas, and it is the body's key blood-sugar–regulating hormone. It is responsible for making sure the levels of sugar in our blood do not surge too high or fall too low.

How does insulin regulate blood sugar? The process begins after we eat. Our bodies digest food and break it down into tiny components. One of these components is glucose, a type of sugar. Blood sugar levels rise after we eat, and normally the elevated blood glucose triggers the release of insulin. Insulin takes hold of glucose in the blood and brings it to cells throughout our body. The hormone is often likened to a key, because it attaches to receptors on cells and "unlocks" them so that glucose can flow inside. Once inside cells, glucose is used as energy or stored to be used as an energy source when needed. Levels of blood glucose eventually fall, and the process begins anew after our next meal or snack.

However, in people with type 2 diabetes, the process of clearing sugar from the blood and feeding it to cells does not work properly, because the cells of people with diabetes have become insulin-resistant. This means that cells fail to respond to insulin's command to unlock and allow glucose to enter. As a result, levels of glucose and insulin in the blood remain high. This is a dangerous condition, because elevated blood glucose can, over many years, raise the body's risk of serious medical complications, including heart disease, kidney damage, stroke, blindness, and even leg and foot amputations. On another level, too much insulin in the blood is associated with obesity and heart disease.

Type 2 diabetes cannot be cured; in other words, once you are diagnosed you will have it for the rest of your life. The good news is that you can manage your disease so that your risk of medical complications is minimal. Managing your diabetes means keeping your blood glucose levels within a certain range through medication, lifestyle habits such as a healthy eating plan and regular exercise, or a combination of drugs and lifestyle changes.

Some people control their diabetes with medication, and there are a number of different types on the market that work in different ways to keep your blood glucose within a normal range. But as with all drugs, anti-diabetes medications come with side effects and risks. This is one reason why some diabetics opt to control their disease by making positive changes in their diet and exercise habits, rather than relying primarily on medication. They follow a balanced eating plan and lose weight if necessary, since excess body weight can contribute to the body's inability to use insulin. Finally, they commit to a regular exercise program. Studies have shown that exercise has many benefits when it comes to controlling diabetes. It can help you lose weight, control cholesterol levels, and lower blood pressure. It can also lower blood levels of insulin and make your cells more responsive to the insulin—this is a direct result of losing fat and gaining muscle from exercising properly.

At this point, you may want to know more about the lifestyle route to controlling your disease, and specifically what to eat. But before getting into the specifics of how certain foods can affect your diabetes, I would like to offer a brief lesson in nutrition that highlights the starring role of carbohydrates.

What Is a Carbohydrate, and How Does It Affect Me?

All foods are made up of protein, fat, and carbohydrates. Foods can contain a single nutrient, but more often they are made of some combination of the three. Each of these nutrients has a vital role to play. Protein helps us grow and allows our bodies to repair themselves when injured. Fat is the best source of energy, because there are more calories inside each gram (9 calories per gram of fat compared with 4 calories in a gram of protein or carbohydrate), but too much of the wrong kinds of fat can pack on pounds and clog your arteries.

If you are reading this book, then you or someone close to you probably has type 2 diabetes. Therefore, you are probably most concerned with carbohydrates, and rightly so. Carbohydrates are the main source of energy for your body and brain. Have you ever taken an exam or gone to work on an empty stomach? You probably felt a bit fuzzy because your brain was not getting the energy it needed. We all need some carbohydrates to function at our best and stay healthy.

The flip side is that a diet rich in certain types of carbohydrates can undermine your efforts to keep your blood sugar on an even level. That is because when digested, carbohydrates such as potatoes, jelly beans, or a bowl of white rice enter your blood rapidly as glucose—the sugar that causes so many problems for diabetics. Foods that consist predominantly of protein and fat may contain glucose, but these nutrients slow down how much is released into your blood. This is one reason why people with diabetes often limit the amount of carbohydrate-containing foods they eat each day.

Another reason to restrict carbohydrates is that certain types of carbohydrate-containing foods (specifically, refined or processed snack foods) can increase levels of triglycerides, a type of fat in your blood that raises your risk of heart disease. And if you have diabetes, you are already at risk for heart disease. A diet that is too high in carbohydrates—specifically, the processed or refined varieties—can make you fat. And as mentioned earlier, people who are overweight are often less responsive to the insulin they produce.

Finally, the unhealthy carbohydrates that many people tend to eat a lot of are precisely those that are high in calories and short on nutrients, as well as being devoid of fiber (a heart-healthy component of whole-grain foods that may lower your risk of certain cancers). Fiber can also give you a feeling of fullness, so you stop eating before you have devoured too many calories. Fiber can therefore be a handy tool if you are trying to lose weight.

But before you completely swear off carbohydrates, keep in mind that not all carbohydrate-containing foods are the same. There are in fact two types of carbohydrates—*refined* and *complex*.

Refined Carbohydrates

Don't let the name fool you into thinking that these foods are well-mannered when it comes to your health. Refined carbohydrates, also called processed carbohydrates, have been stripped of their nutrients and fiber and manufactured into snacks, sugary cereals, white bread, and white rice, among other common food items. These foods are generally high in calories, sugar, and trans-fatty acids, which can raise your cholesterol. Food manufacturers use these ingredients because they allow food to remain in your pantry unspoiled for a long period of time (years, in some instances).

Complex Carbohydrates

These carbohydrates are foods that have been processed minimally, if at all. Complex carbohydrates include bulgur, barley, legumes (kidney beans, black beans, lima beans, garbanzo beans, and lentils, among others), fresh fruits and vegetables, and whole-grain cereals and breads. Complex carbohydrates are superior when it comes to nutrition, and they are loaded with heart-healthy fiber.

For our purposes, the main distinction between refined and complex carbohydrates is their effect on blood sugar. Refined carbohydrates release glucose into the bloodstream almost immediately. Shortly after you consume refined carbohydrates, your blood glucose rises sharply, and you may feel a surge of energy. To match this rapid rise, your pancreas churns out large amounts of insulin. For people who do not have diabetes, blood sugar levels return to normal because insulin has done its job. But for people with diabetes, a surge of sugar and insulin into the blood can sabotage your efforts to control the disease with food alone.

Complex carbohydrates also release glucose into the blood, but they do so at a slower and steadier rate. This is because it takes the body longer to digest complex carbohydrates. As a result, your body makes less insulin because it does not have to deal with as much glucose in your blood at one time, which leads to a more moderate release of glucose and insulin. With the help of the recipes in this book, you will be headed on a clear and delicious path to controlling your disease.

What Is the Glycemic Index, and How Can I Use It?

How quickly a carbohydrate-containing food releases sugar into the blood is so important for people with diabetes that health care professionals have developed a ranking of foods based on this property. This ranking is known as a food's glycemic index, or GI. The glycemic index measures the effect of carbohydrates on our blood sugar levels.

Foods with a high glycemic index cause blood sugars to rise quickly. Dramatic spikes in blood sugar lead to high insulin levels, which (as mentioned previously) have been linked to obesity, heart disease, and diabetes. Foods with a low glycemic index will cause glucose to be released in a slow and steady manner, and as a result, blood levels of glucose and insulin do not rise too high.

Researchers determine a food's GI against white bread, which is assigned a GI value of 100. If a certain food raised average blood sugar by half as much as the white bread did, it would receive a GI value of 50. There are several books on the market that offer more details on the glycemic index and provide a ranking of foods. Some health professionals are advocating that a food's GI be listed on nutrition labels alongside calories, grams of fat, and other nutritional information.

Critics point out that the GI can be hard to understand if it is not consistent. For one, the effect of a food on blood sugar depends on whether it is eaten alone or as part of a meal. Eating a meal or snack that is nutritionally balanced—that is, contains the right amounts of protein, fat, and carbohydrates—will slow down the rate at which sugar is released into your blood. Besides the nutrient mix of a meal, the method used to cook a dish can affect a food's GI value. For example, adding acid such as vinegar or tomato sauce to a recipe can lower the GI of a food.

Despite these criticisms, some dietitians and doctors believe that when used as a general guideline, the glycemic index ranking can still be helpful for people with diabetes as well as for those trying to lose weight. In other words, base your diets on foods with a low GI. Eat medium-GI foods occasionally and high-GI foods only rarely. If you look at which foods fall into each category, it makes a lot of nutritional sense—foods with a low glycemic index ranking include complex carbohydrates such as barley, lentils, and All-Bran cereal, along with many beans and some fruits and vegetables.

How Can I Control My Disease Through Diet?

The word *diet* is normally very misunderstood. Its root lies in the Greek language, where *dieta* means "a manner of life." In other words, a diet is a way of life. Unfortunately, most people think of a diet not as a way of life but as an eating regimen that is endured for a period of time in order to reach a desired goal and then abandoned in favor of the old eating habits that will get you into trouble once again. To avoid any confusion, I will refer instead to what you can do to control your diabetes as an "eating plan." Ideally, the plan you devise will be a long-term one. It should be sustainable and flexible, include a wide variety of foods that provide all the nutrients you need to feel your best, and satisfy your body's food cravings.

The goal is not as complicated as it sounds. Nor is it overly restrictive, because no particular food need be off-limits. To do this successfully, it is necessary that the majority of foods you eat be nutrient-dense (meaning they are full of vitamins and minerals) but low or moderate in calories and fat. But your plan should also accommodate an occasional splurge so that you can still enjoy all of the delicacies you savored before being diagnosed with diabetes. The difference now is that your level of awareness about food and its immediate effect on your blood sugar is most important. Learning how to spread out your carbohydrates over the course of the day and to make choices—bread or dessert, for instance—can keep you on the right track.

There is no single diabetes diet that applies to everyone affected by the disease. You chart your own course by making individual choices based on your food preferences, schedule, exercise habits, and genetic profile.

Nutrition knowledge, moderation, and flexibility are the main components of a healthy eating plan that can help you to manage your diabetes while still enjoying delicious food. Below are some tips to help you select foods and create your own eating plan.

Look at the Whole Pie

Imagine that all the foods you eat in the course of a day fit on a huge plate. Now, group these foods according to the primary nutrient they contain (protein, fat, or carbohydrates). Tally up what percentage comes from each nutrient.

According to the American Diabetes Association, protein should account for roughly 10 to 20 percent of your daily intake of nutrients, fat about 30 percent, and carbohydrates about 50 to 60 percent. Some doctors and dietitians counsel clients to reduce their intake of carbohydrates even further, to about 40 percent of total calories. It is generally agreed that a low-carbohydrate diet is one in which 40 percent or less of total calories comes from carbohydrate-containing foods.

If you decide to restrict your carbohydrates below the lower recommended threshold of 50 percent, you might want to consult your doctor or a registered dietitian, who can help you formulate a plan. Cutting back too drastically on carbohydrates, especially the healthy kinds, can deprive you of the nutrients your body needs to function at its best. Later on in this chapter, we will discuss which vitamins and minerals your body needs, and where you can get them.

Remember that Calories Still Count

Less than a decade ago, "fat-free" was all the rage. Products that were stripped of fat (only to be bumped up with sugar, a refined carbohydrate) hit the grocery store shelves and sold like (fat-free) hotcakes. Today the tables have turned, and retailers probably could not get those same products to sell—unless, of course, they were stripped of all their carbohydrates.

The bottom line is this: the popularity of weight-loss diets waxes and wanes, but through each fad calories do count. If you eat more calories than you use each day, you will create a calorie surplus that will show up on the scale over time. This is true regardless of which nutrient delivers your calories. Using up more calories than you consume by staying active, choosing healthy foods, and limiting your intake of rich desserts and snack foods can help you lose weight if you need to, or else maintain a healthy weight level.

Be Picky About Protein

Like carbohydrate-containing foods, sources of protein are not all the same. Some types of protein are rich in fat, especially the saturated type, which can raise your cholesterol and put you at risk for heart disease. Many people with diabetes already have high cholesterol. What's more, having diabetes means you are already at risk for heart disease. Limiting protein foods that contain saturated fat is therefore wise. Specific foods to avoid or limit include high-fat cheese, processed sandwich meats, pork sausage, bacon, and spareribs.

Instead, choose lean sources of protein such as white-meat chicken or turkey without the skin; fish and shellfish; low-fat cheese, yogurt, and milk; and lean beef, pork loin, lamb, and veal.

Opt for Healthy Fats

Anyone would do well to cut down on saturated fat and cholesterol and instead eat more of the healthy unsaturated fats found in foods such as olives, avocados, nuts, and fish. But if you have diabetes, the reasons to replace artery-clogging fats with the healthy kinds are more immediate.

For one, saturated fat in animal foods such as beef, whole milk, and full-fat cheese raises blood cholesterol, which is a major risk factor for heart disease. As I have already noted, simply by having diabetes you are already at risk for heart disease, which is the leading cause of death among Americans. To lower levels of saturated fat in your diet, choose lean cuts of meat, remove skin and all visible fat from meat and poultry before cooking, buy low-fat milk and other dairy products, and try grilling your food, which will get rid of some of the fat.

Another type of fat you will want to avoid is trans fat, also called trans-fatty acids or hydrogenated fat. Trans fat is a processed fat found in snack foods such as cakes, cookies and crackers, as well as some types of margarine. Like saturated fat, trans fat raises your cholesterol and LDL cholesterol (commonly called "bad" cholesterol). But trans fat has another effect: it lowers your HDL cholesterol, the "good" cholesterol that you want to remain high in your body.

Monounsaturated fats, on the other hand, are heart-healthy. These fats have the potential to lower your total cholesterol and your "bad" cholesterol, and raise your "good" cholesterol. To incorporate these fats into your diet, replace peanut oil and shortening with canola oil and olive oil, add a handful of raw, unsalted walnuts to salads, cereal, and stir-fries, or slice an avocado into a salad or use it in place of mayonnaise.

Choose Carbohydrates Carefully

I have already discussed the effects that different carbohydrate-containing foods have on your blood sugar, your weight, and your risk of heart disease. Still, I am going to repeat it now, because the message is so important: make your carbohydrates complex ones! Include vegetables, fruits, and whole grains in your diet.

Some words of caution when buying bread: be sure to check the ingredient list to make sure the first ingredient reads "whole grain" or "whole wheat." This means that the bread was made predominantly from the entire wheat kernel, including the bran, which provides fiber and the germ, as well as the essential vitamin E and the mineral selenium. Do not be fooled by bread that is made from "wheat flour" or that is labeled "multigrain" or "twelve-grain." These breads contain more white flour than anything else.

You should also space your carbohydrates out throughout the day. Discuss with your doctor or a registered dietitian how many servings of carbohydrates you are allowed each day and how best to allocate them. This will depend on how many calories you eat per day, whether you are taking medication, if you exercise, and other factors. In general, you should have some type of carbohydrate at each meal and snack. This can help keep your blood sugar in check and provide your muscles and brain with a regular stream of glucose.

Beware of Foods That Are Labeled "Low-Fat" or "Fat-Free"

Products labeled "low-fat," "nonfat," or "fat-free" may seem healthy, but they often have extra salt and sugar (read: carbohydrates) lurking inside. This is because when the fat is taken out of a product, the manufacturer usually adds salt and sugar to improve the taste. And these foods are usually processed, so you will want to avoid them in the first place. Check the grams of carbohydrates on the Nutrition Facts label and make some comparisons. You will find that full-fat foods can be lower in total calories, as well as in grams of carbohydrates.

Can I Eat Fruit?

Many of today's popular low-carbohydrate diets recommend that people with diabetes, and anyone trying to lose weight, should limit their consumption of fruit or give it up entirely. That is because fruits are full of sugar. However, the type of sugar that most fruit contains is fructose. Unlike glucose, fructose enters the blood more slowly and does not cause a rush of insulin.

Fruit has other benefits. It contains fiber along with vitamins and minerals that can cut your risk for several chronic diseases and boost your immunity. People with diabetes should include fruit in their healthy eating plan. However, some fruits are better than others when it comes to their effect on blood sugar. Some of the best bets are apples, berries (all kinds), cherries, grapefruits, grapes, oranges, pears, and plums. Tropical fruits such as bananas, pineapples, and mangoes are very high in sugar and should be eaten in moderation. Likewise, fruit juice is almost pure sugar. If you want some fruit juice in your diet, water it down with seltzer and drink it only occasionally.

Are There Any Foods That Are Particularly Healthy for People with Diabetes?

In general, foods that are healthy for everyone are also good for people with diabetes. There are some preliminary studies suggesting that some foods may have positive effects on blood glucose and insulin levels. These are fish, nuts, coffee, cinnamon, and soy.

Fish

Fish is a lean source of protein, and some types are rich in omega-3 fatty acids. These fats are good for the heart and, according to a study published in *Circulation* in 2003, the benefits appear to be even more significant in women with type 2 diabetes. Fish that are rich in omega-3 fatty acids include salmon, sardines, and tuna.

Nuts

Research has shown that nuts and other foods that are rich in the mineral magnesium, such as grains and leafy green vegetables, may help your body protect against developing type 2 diabetes. That may be because unsaturated fats, such as those found in certain nuts including walnuts and almonds, may improve the body's ability to use insulin and regulate blood glucose.

Take note, however: nuts are still high in fat and calories, and adding nuts to your usual eating plan can contribute excess calories and cause you to gain weight—a risk factor for both diabetes and heart disease. So if you decide to add more nuts to your diet, be sure you do so as a substitute for other foods such as meat or refined grain products.

Coffee

The latest research on coffee, published in the *Annals of Internal Medicine* and the *Journal of the American Medical Association* in March 2004, suggests that the world's most popular beverage may actually help to ward off type 2 diabetes. Caffeine, which increases heart rate and burns calories, may be the reason. Or it could be that caffeinated coffee contains compounds (magnesium, potassium, and some antioxidants) that may help to keep blood sugar in check.

While the findings are surely exciting to coffee aficionados, keep in mind that the research on coffee and diabetes is still in the early stages.

Try to limit your coffee intake to roughly three cups a day, especially if you find that a cup in the afternoon prevents you from getting a good night's sleep. People with hypertension (high blood pressure) should also be careful, since too much coffee can raise your blood pressure.

Cinnamon

A study reported in *Diabetes Care* in 2003 suggests that adding a dash of cinnamon to your frothy cup of coffee each morning may be an additional bonus when it comes to controlling your diabetes—the spice may contain compounds that can help the body use insulin.

Soy

Soy is a low-fat protein source that you can enjoy in several ways: soybeans, tofu, or tempeh. Soy products can be firm and used in stir-fries, or silken and used for sauces and frozen drinks. Whatever form it takes, soy is associated with a lower risk of cholesterol and heart disease. Soy may also ward off the risk factors of heart disease and kidney disease in people with diabetes who eat soy in place of animal protein, a study published in the *European Journal of Clinical Nutrition* in 2003 suggests.

In another study, reported in *Diabetes Care* in 2002, older women with diabetes who took a daily soy supplement showed improvements in blood sugar control and had lower blood insulin levels.

Can I Eat Dessert?

Even with diabetes, you can still enjoy desserts, even a rich chocolate cake or a buttery tarte Tatin, so long as you let moderation be your guide.

Moderation involves keeping an eye on the amount you eat, how often you indulge, and how a dessert fits in with your overall eating plan for the day. If you decide before the meal that you want to order dessert, then forgo other carbohydrates. If you are dining out, skip the bread and butter and ask if you can substitute extra vegetables for the potato or rice that comes with the meal. If you are entertaining or dining at someone else's house and don't want to offend your host, take small bites of everything—including dessert. Often a bite or two is enough to satisfy a post-dinner craving for something sweet. Sharing a dessert and limiting the number of times each week that you indulge can also help keep your eating plan on track without being overly restrictive.

But for many people, dessert can be a slippery slope. One bite leads to another and another, until before you realize it the plate is empty! For this reason, many people with diabetes find it easier to skip dessert altogether. If you think that a bite or two will be too difficult, order a skim cappuccino or a cup of tea if you are in a restaurant, or prepare a satisfying beverage at home. Chai, a black tea brewed with spices, honey, and milk, can be very satisfying; it is available with or without caffeine, and is sold in supermarkets.

What About Alcohol?

Like desserts, alcohol can be a part of your eating plan as long as you make the appropriate adjustments and drink in moderation. For diabetics, moderation means no more than one drink per day for women and no more than two drinks a day for men. A drink is equal to about 12 ounces of beer, 5 ounces of wine, or 1½ ounces of hard alcohol such as vodka, gin, or whiskey.

If you drink, beware that alcohol can undermine your resolve to follow a healthy eating plan. After just one drink, you might feel less inhibited and end up making some choices that sabotage your weight loss or healthy eating plan, leaving you feeling bad about yourself the next day. Also, be sure to have your drink with food and not on an empty stomach. Drinking alcohol when you have not eaten for several hours can cause people with diabetes to experience hypoglycemia (dangerously low blood sugar). When this occurs, your body and brain do not get the fuel they need. You may sweat, feel ravenous or anxious, develop a rapid heartbeat, or turn pale. You may also develop a headache or double vision, have trouble concentrating, or feel incredibly tired.

Also, be sure to sip your drink slowly. Check your blood sugar before you take your first sip and again before going to bed, since alcohol can cause hypoglycemia for up to twelve hours after drinking. Finally, be sure to have a snack that will bring your blood sugar to a normal range (between 100 to 140 mg/dl) if it is low.

Which Vitamins and Minerals Do I Need?

The vitamin and mineral needs of people with diabetes are no different than those of individuals without the disease. An eating plan that follows the guidelines listed in the preceding pages—one that includes lean sources of protein, low-fat dairy products, healthy fats, whole grains and other sources of fiber, and plenty of fruits and vegetables—is varied enough to give you the vitamins and minerals you need. There is no need to invest in a computer or software that tallies micrograms (mcg) of nutrients in this food or international units (IU) of nutrients in that recipe. Below is a list of the main vitamins and minerals you need, what you need them for, and where you can get them.

VITAMIN	WHERE TO GET IT	WHY YOU NEED IT
Vitamin A	Green leafy vegetables, milk, cantaloupe, apricots	Healthy skin and bones
Vitamin B_1 (thiamin)	Whole-grain cereals, meat	Helps convert carbohydrates into energy
Vitamin B_2 (riboflavin)	Green vegetables, fish, milk, cheese	Helps to metabolize food
Niacin	Fish, meat, nuts, legumes	Helps the body use energy from food
Vitamin B_6 (pyridoxine)	Liver, yeast	Used by body for growth and development
Vitamin B_{12} (cobalamin)	Meat, other animal foods	Used by nervous system and red blood cells
Folate	Green leafy vegetables, oranges	Used by nervous system and red blood cells
Vitamin C	Citrus fruits, potatoes	Used by your immune system

VITAMIN	WHERE TO GET IT	WHY YOU NEED IT
Vitamin D	Fortified dairy products; also made by skin exposed to sun	Helps the body absorb calcium; therefore, necessary for strong bones
Vitamin E	Whole grains, vegetable oils	An antioxidant that boosts immunity
Vitamin K	Leafy vegetables	Helps the blood to clot

MINERAL	WHERE TO GET IT	WHY YOU NEED IT
Calcium	Milk and dairy products	Helps to build strong bones; used for cardiac function
Iodine	Added to some table salt	Aids in production of thyroid hormones
Iron	Meat	Needed for red blood cells (which transport oxygen throughout the body)
Magnesium	Milk, dairy, vegetables	Builds bones and teeth
Phosphorus	Milk, dairy, vegetables	Builds bones and teeth
Potassium	Fruits, vegetables, meat	Regulates water balance in body
Sodium	Most foods	Regulates water balance in body
Zinc	Meat, liver, eggs	Helps the body to use insulin

Can Artificial Sweeteners Help Me Control My Diabetes?

Many people with diabetes forgo table sugar for one of the artificial sweeteners on the market today. These products are much sweeter than table sugar (sucrose). Some do not contain any calories, while others are not absorbed by the body and therefore do not have any effect on blood glucose levels. However, these products can come with side effects that range from a bitter aftertaste to diarrhea and bloating if consumed in excess. Also keep in mind that some cannot be used for cooking or baking.

The following list includes all of the artificial sweeteners on the market today.

Acesulfame Potassium

This sweetener is also known as Ace-K, Sunette, and Sweet One. It is a synthetic chemical that is twice as sweet as table sugar and contains 4 calories per gram (the same amount as table sugar or sucrose). However, since our bodies cannot break down the chemical, it passes through the digestive system unabsorbed and does not contribute calories to the diet. It is used in baked goods, frozen desserts, candy, and drinks because it remains stable when heated.

Aspartame

Aspartame is the generic name for NutraSweet, NutraTaste, and Equal, and is found in many processed foods. It is about twice as sweet as sucrose and does not have an unpleasant aftertaste. Aspartame is made by combining the amino acids aspartic acid and phenylalanine, and so people with the rare inherited disorder phenylketonuria, who are not able to break down the amino acid phenylalanine, should avoid this sugar substitute.

Saccharin

Saccharin is the generic name for Sweet'n Low. It has a distinct aftertaste that is sometimes described as bitter or metallic. Saccharin is a synthetic chemical that is three times sweeter than regular table sugar and is not metabolized by the body.

Stevia

You will not find this sweetener, also known as sweet leaf and honey leaf, in the grocery store or as an ingredient in processed food. That is because the U.S. Food and Drug Administration does not allow stevia to be used in food. Instead, it is sold as a dietary supplement and can be found in your local health food store. Stevia comes from a plant that grows in Brazil and Paraguay. Like other artificial sweeteners, it cannot be absorbed by your body.

Sucralose

Sucralose, or Splenda, is used in baked goods, drinks, and frozen desserts, as well as a general tabletop sweetener. It is made by combining sucrose (table sugar) with chlorine. Sucralose is used in several dessert recipes in this book, including Splenda Panna Cotta (page 160) and Mango and Avocado Carpaccio (page 164).

Sugar Alcohols

Sugar alcohols are made by combining hydrogen with natural sugars such as sucrose or glucose. They do not raise blood sugar as quickly as sugar and are not well absorbed by the body. However, they may cause diarrhea, bloating, and gas if consumed in excess. A product contains a sugar alcohol if you see any of the following names in the ingredient list: xylitol, erythritol, isomalt, lactitol, maltitol, mannitol, sorbitol, or hydrogenated starch hydrolysates.

Diabetes and Delicious Food

If you have read this chapter from start to finish, you may find yourself saturated with information. The point is not to remember everything in the preceding pages, however—you can always come back and use this chapter as a reference guide. The message to take with you on your journey through the rest of the book, as well as through your daily life, is that diabetes and delicious food are natural partners. Armed with this nutrition knowledge, you will be ready to take charge of your health and enjoy every future bite.

SUZANNE ROSTLER, M.S., R.D.

The Diabetic Chef

Introduction

I want to tell you a little bit about myself and why I decided to write this book. First of all, I am a professional chef at a high-end restaurant in New York City. I also happen to have type 2 diabetes.

My Life as a Cook

In 1993, I earned a degree from the Culinary Institute of America (CIA) in Hyde Park, New York. I went on to work as the executive chef of several critically acclaimed New York City restaurants, including Trinity, Capitale, Local, and Cucina. While I was at Capitale, it was named a Best New Restaurant by *Esquire* magazine. My new American style of cooking has also been praised by the *New York Times* and *New York* magazine.

However, I wasn't always such an accomplished chef. Young cooks are notorious for trying to do more than they are capable of, and when I first started working in a professional kitchen, I wasn't any different.

I began as a prep cook at the age of fourteen, performing such menial tasks as chopping carrots, slicing potatoes, and dicing onions. When I was nineteen, I was chosen by my fraternity brothers at Brooklyn College (where I majored in speech and public communications) to prepare food for the annual Country Fair held on campus every spring. I thought I was ready for the challenge, but boy, was I wrong! I decided to make crab cakes and barbecued ribs for our booth. Fifty pounds of crab cakes and two hundred ribs later, there was crab everywhere—on my mother's kitchen ceiling, the walls, you name it—and an oven filled with ribs that were burnt black and completely inedible.

But that was nothing compared to the summer I spent at Hunter's Run, a restaurant in Boynton Beach, Florida, after graduating from the CIA. I was a young hotshot with some professional experience under my belt, and I thought I knew everything. There was a sous chef named Moe who was tough on me because I was so arrogant, and he decided to teach me the lesson of a lifetime. One day he gave me a huge amount of prep work to do, from shucking bushels of clams and oysters to chopping up mounds of vegetables for dinner that night. I was falling way behind, so I decided to take a shortcut. I put most of the oysters in the freezer to cool down, which makes them easier to open. My plan was to work on one bushel while the rest were cooling. The only problem was, all the oysters froze to death and had to be thrown away. I didn't lose my job, but as punishment I had to spend the rest of the summer doing prep work.

I also learned a valuable lesson: do not try to do too many things at once in the kitchen. When young cooks start to work for me, I always tell them to finish one task all the way through, and only then should they move on to the next job. Until you are comfortable multitasking in the kitchen, it is best not to attempt it, because you can start off preparing a nice home-cooked meal and end up having to order in pizza (as well as costing yourself a lot of money in wasted food). There might even be an angry sous chef named Moe looking for you.

The recipes in this cookbook are designed to allow home cooks to move easily from one step to the next. Even the most difficult dishes can be broken down into a series of small steps, resulting in a finished product that you will be amazed came from your own kitchen.

Living with Diabetes

Like many of those who suffer from diabetes, it is a disease that runs in my family. My great-grandmother died of complications from diabetes, my grandmother went blind from it, and my father, mother, and uncle all have it. So it wasn't a huge surprise when I too was diagnosed with diabetes.

While I was still a child, my doctor discovered I had high triglycerides, a type of fat that accumulates in the blood and is a risk factor for diabetes. It didn't help that I grew up in a Jewish family in Brooklyn, where food such as lox, eggs, whitefish salad, bagels, brisket, and pizza were the norm. All of these things taste great, but none is particularly healthy for diabetics.

Of course, being young also meant I was stubborn, and I thought I could get away with any kind of lifestyle I chose. So there I was, a 240-pound chef stuffing my face with everything from frog's legs to foie gras, eating my way through every kitchen, and enjoying life without a care in the world.

Inevitably, my luck ran out. In 1996, I was cooking in Italy on the private yacht of an American business mogul, and I began getting severely seasick. Not realizing that I was a diabetic, I treated my nausea with Coca-Cola and ginger ale. For ten days and nights I couldn't see straight, and I knew something was seriously wrong.

Back on dry land, I made an appointment with my doctor. It soon became clear that I had what I always secretly feared—type 2 diabetes. My blood sugar registered a whopping 350. The doctor immediately put me on medication, and I was forced to severely limit my caloric intake. Imagine being a twenty-seven-year-old aspiring chef and being told to stay away from fat and simple carbohydrates! I thought my career was over. How could I cook if I couldn't taste? And how could I help support my new fiancée and our yet unborn children?

Rather than despair, I immediately set out to do whatever it took to control my diabetes. I cut out simple carbohydrates from my diet—no more Coca-Cola or Frosted Flakes—and balanced my intake of carbohydrates, protein, and fat; within a month I had dropped 40 pounds. In 1997, my wife, Jennifer, and I were married, and today we live in Queens with our two young children.

My newfound discipline carried over to my work. I transformed my cooking style by cutting down on fat and carbohydrates, and today my recipes combine simple ingredients in a way that anyone at home can replicate. With my diabetes under control, it was also perfectly safe for me to taste the dishes I was preparing, so I could ensure that my food would be appealing to everyone who ate at my restaurant.

My Cooking Philosophy

When creating a dish, I focus on three things: the needs of my guests, maintaining the integrity of the main ingredient I am working with, and making sure the central component of a particular dish fits naturally with all the other ingredients on the plate. If a guest at my restaurant orders chicken, he or she should taste chicken, and whatever else is accompanying it should play a supporting role without overwhelming the palate.

I encourage you to take what you learn from this book and create something new based on the foods you like. However, that does not mean forcing ingredients together that do not seem natural; if a recipe does not sound appealing on paper, chances are it will not work on the plate.

I think the quality of ingredients should be more important than anything else when preparing a dish. Ask this question: can you eat a piece of grilled fish that is seasoned only with salt and pepper and still be satisfied? That does not mean the fish has to be served that way, but at least you are starting off with something worth adding to. On the other hand, I do not believe in forcing ingredients together if they are not meant to be.

If nothing else, I hope that anyone using this cookbook will learn to embrace this approach. Look for the freshest ingredients available, and examine all your products closely to determine their quality before purchasing them. If possible, spend a little more money for top-quality ingredients, and you will be rewarded with better-tasting and ultimately more satisfying dishes.

Eating Your Way to a Healthy Diet

While carbohydrates and fat are necessary parts of a diabetic diet, it is important to keep their levels under control. (It is generally recommended that people with diabetes get about 50 percent of their calories from carbohydrates, 30 percent from fat, and 20 percent from protein;

however, this does not hold true for all diabetics, so be sure to consult your doctor before starting a new eating plan.) To keep the amount of fat in my recipes at a minimal level, I rely primarily on healthful cooking methods such as grilling, poaching, and sautéing.

In addition, I avoid using refined sugars whenever possible. If you can find raw products that are naturally sweet, such as ripe peaches in the middle of July, you will be able to satisfy your cravings in a healthy way. This brings me to another important aspect of cooking that many people do not pay attention to today: do not purchase foods out of season! There's just no reason for it; every time you do, not only are you likely to end up with an inferior product, but you are also probably paying top dollar for it.

Culinary Influences

My main culinary influences are Asian and French, but Italian and Mediterranean cuisine also play a big part in my repertoire and in this cookbook.

I find Asian food to be very simple and clean, with a focus on one main ingredient, and this is the way I approach everything in my cooking. I think there always needs to be a central ingredient in a dish, and everything else should support and show it off. Whether you are talking about Vietnamese, Chinese, Korean, Thai, or Japanese cuisine, this philosophy holds true, but I find Japanese to be the purest cuisine of all, and the one that I am most influenced by.

Every chef I have ever worked with has had the same fascination with Asian ingredients, starting with my early days at Mesa Grill in Manhattan. New York City (and especially Brooklyn, where I live) is a melting pot for all cuisines. Visiting neighborhoods such as Chinatown, I see so many new and unusual ingredients that I can try at a restaurant or buy from an Asian grocery and experiment with.

However, French technique was what I was taught in cooking school and at the restaurants I worked in when I was younger, and to this day I apply it to everything I do. There is a level of refinement associated with French restaurants, and for many people there is the perception that it is the world's greatest cuisine.

Everything begins with how we purchase our ingredients. Are you going to buy fish, meat, and vegetables that are old, or food that is fresh and tasty? Ultimately, you always want to look for the best quality possible, so that you have to do the least to it to bring out the maximum flavor. French and Asian cuisine strictly adheres to this principle, and Italian, Greek, and other Mediterranean cooking does as well. Take my recipe for Warm Baked Apple with Golden Raisins and Walnuts (page 159) in the dessert section—I start off with a fresh, crisp apple and turn it into a great dessert by adding nuts and raisins and roasting it to bring out the fruit's natural sweetness without the addition of any refined sugars. The results are more than satisfying.

Everything in Moderation

I truly believe that the diabetic food plan is the perfect diet for everyone, not just diabetics. As clichéd as it may sound, the old saying "Everything in moderation" is great advice to follow when creating an eating plan to control your diabetes. And with the recipes found in this cookbook, you will not feel as if you are missing out on anything that "normal" people enjoy. In fact, my cooking style is the same when I prepare food for myself or for guests at my restaurant—I limit carbohydrates, use primarily healthy fats such as olive oil and canola oil, and feature a menu filled with vegetables, fish, and poultry dishes, along with meat in moderate amounts.

Cooking is less about time and recipes than it is about feeling the food and absorbing its flavor. If you think a dish needs less salt than the recipe calls for, use less salt; in other words, do not be afraid to rely on your instincts, even if it means not following a recipe to the letter.

My philosophy for life is the same as in the kitchen: if something doesn't go exactly the way you planned, do not get discouraged, and never give up. I am proof that life is not over if you have diabetes. In fact, it is just beginning. So let's cook our way to a healthier lifestyle, and have fun doing it. Enjoy!

Chapter 1

Techniques and Equipment

The techniques and equipment described in this chapter are found in recipes throughout the book. They are all commonly used in professional kitchens and can be easily replicated by the home cook. If you have trouble finding equipment and food items called for in this book, do not despair: Websites filled with gourmet foods and cooking supplies abound on the Internet. Among the more elaborate ones are www.cooking.com, www.williamssonoma.com, and www.epicurious. com.

Blanching and Shocking

Professional chefs regularly use this method to prepare firm vegetables such as broccoli, asparagus, and carrots, and I have included it in recipes throughout the book. First the vegetables are *blanched,* or cooked in a large pot of boiling water until they begin to tenderize, usually from 2 to 4 minutes. They are then removed and immediately *shocked* in a large bowl of ice water; this stops the cooking process and retains the desired texture and color of the vegetables. Once the vegetables are cold, they should be removed from the ice water and set aside. When a dish is ready to be served, the vegetables can be briefly sautéed in a small amount of butter or oil before plating.

Cheesecloth

No professional kitchen is complete without cheesecloth. It is made of woven cotton and can be used to strain impurities from purees, soups, and other liquids such as chicken stock. It is also available in most cookware stores and gourmet food shops, and some supermarkets. Cheesecloth can also be used to make a sachet (see "Sachet," page 14).

Deglazing

After cooking meat and fish, the brown pieces that remain on the bottom of the pan are called *fond*. This fond is packed with flavor, and deglazing the pan creates a simple but delicious sauce. Deglazing is often done with wine or other alcohol such as brandy, but almost any liquid, including chicken stock or even water, will work.

To deglaze, first pour off any leftover fat. Keeping the pan off the heat (especially when using alcohol, which can flare up), pour in approximately ¼ cup of wine or other liquid. Return the pan to a low flame; using a wooden spoon, scrape the fond off the bottom and stir it together with the liquid. Bring the liquid to a simmer and strain through a fine mesh strainer. This basic sauce can also be flavored with additional ingredients such as fresh herbs before straining, as well as thickened with cornstarch or flour.

Fine Mesh Strainer

Strainers of various sizes and shapes are used regularly in professional kitchens to remove solids from sauces and stocks, as well as to make purees silky smooth. In general, the recipes in this book call for using a fine mesh strainer, which is available in most kitchen supply stores and online. To remove even the smallest impurities from soups and stocks, line a fine mesh strainer with cheesecloth before straining (see "Cheesecloth," above).

Juicing

Juicers are used to liquefy raw fruits and vegetables. They range in quality and price from the simplest plastic manual juicer to professional electric extractors costing hundreds of dollars. For fresh lemons, limes, and oranges, an inexpensive plastic model works fine. However, juicing vegetables is a great way to get the vitamins and minerals you need in your diet every day, so it may be worthwhile to pay more for an electric extractor that is strong enough to juice most vegetables, including carrots and celery.

Knife Cuts

Some recipes in the book call for cutting fruits and vegetables into specific sizes, including brunoise, chiffonade, julienne, segments, small dice, medium dice, and large dice. These differ from chopping or mincing, which results in less uniform shapes. By cutting each piece approximately the same size, you ensure that they will finish cooking at the same time.

Brunoise: A brunoise cut is ⅛ inch by ⅛ inch by ⅛ inch. To form a brunoise, first julienne the item (see below), then cut these stick-size pieces perpendicularly to form even squares.

Chiffonade: A chiffonade is the very thinly sliced leaves of such vegetables as basil, mint, or spinach. To prepare, roll the leaves up and cut them across horizontally. It is often used to garnish dishes such as Grilled Halibut and Buckwheat Salad (page 89).

Julienne: The dimension of a julienne stick is typically ⅛ inch by ⅛ inch by 1 inch. To make them, square off the long sides of a carrot, for example, and cut it perpendicularly to form rectangular shapes approximately 1 inch long. Cut these rectangular pieces lengthwise into ⅛-inch slices, then cut the slices again lengthwise to form the proper shape.

Segments: To make citrus segments, first cut off the peel and rind with a knife. Then use a paring knife to remove each segment by cutting on either side of the membranes separating them.

Small dice: This cut is similar to a brunoise, only larger—¼ inch by ¼ inch by ¼ inch—but the method is essentially the same: start off with a larger julienne stick (also called a bâtonnet) that is ¼ inch by ¼ inch by 1 inch, and cut it down to create a small dice.

Medium dice: The method is the same as for a brunoise. A medium dice is ⅜ inch by ⅜ inch by ⅜ inch.

Large dice: Again, the method is the same as for a brunoise. A large dice is ⅝ inch by ⅝ inch by ⅝ inch.

Knife Sharpening

Just as important as owning a high-quality set of knives (see "Knives," below) is making sure your knives are well cared for and kept sharp. A properly sharpened knife is actually less dangerous than a dull one—a sharp blade will go easily through most food items, but a dull knife could slip and cause serious injury.

A dull knife can be sharpened using a whetstone. First wet the stone with water or mineral oil, then run the blade across it at approximately a 20-degree angle. Do this several times on each side until sharp. To maintain the sharpness of a blade as long as possible, always use a cutting board, and occasionally hone the blade with a steel—a long, thin rod.

Knives

I strongly recommend purchasing a good set of knives. They make the preparation of ingredients far easier and more efficient, and if treated properly, they will last a lifetime (see "Knife Sharpening," above). My main weapons of choice in the kitchen are a chef's knife, utility knife, paring knife, and bread knife.

Bread knife: A serrated sawlike knife used for cutting breads. It is also useful in cutting through citrus fruits and tomatoes.

I recommend knives with high-carbon stainless-steel blades. The steel keeps the knife strong, and the carbon makes it easier to sharpen. Another option is a blade made exclusively of carbon steel, which is ideal for preparing sushi and other delicate foods that require a thin, razor-sharp blade.

Chef's knife: The blade of a chef's knife ranges in size from 8 to 14 inches long. It can be used for everything from chopping carrots, slicing tomatoes, and dicing onions to deboning fish and poultry.

Utility knife: A utility knife is a smaller, narrower version of a chef's knife, with a 6- to 8-inch blade. It is useful for more delicate cutting jobs, such as mincing shallots and garlic.

Paring knife: Paring knives are 2 to 4 inches long. They are best for performing detailed cutting work, such as coring tomatoes or halving grapes.

Meat Mallet

This tool is used to pound cutlets thin, which helps tenderize the meat and allows it to cook more quickly and evenly. Place a piece of meat (or fish) between two pieces of plastic wrap and lightly pound until the desired thickness is achieved. Chicken, veal, and pork cutlets all benefit from this method.

Mandoline

Mandolines are used to slice, shred, and grate vegetables such as cucumbers and radishes into thin, even pieces. Adjustable blades also allow for the creation of julienne strips, french fries, and waffle cuts (as in waffle-cut potato chips). The traditional French mandoline is made of stainless steel and is equipped with a hand guard. Japanese mandolines have become much more popular in recent years; made of plastic with a metal blade, they are lighter and less expensive than the French model, and I find they are often easier to use.

Pans

There is seemingly no end to the number of pans available today in kitchen supply stores such as Williams-Sonoma and Crate & Barrel and on the Internet. But for the purposes of this cookbook, all you really need is a 10- to 12-inch stainless-steel sauté pan, a high-quality nonstick sauté pan, and possibly a grill pan.

Grill pan: Outdoor grilling is often fun and rewarding, but in areas where it gets cold in the winter, cooking outside is not always a possibility. While a grill pan will not be able to replicate the flavor of meat, fish, and vegetables that are grilled outdoors using natural woods or charcoal, it will be possible to reproduce the signature crosshatch markings associated with grilling.

Sauté pan: When purchasing a sauté pan, go for quality rather than trying to save a few bucks. Properly cared for, a heavy-bottomed stainless-steel sauté pan from a reputable company will last you a lifetime. I am particularly fond of All-Clad cookware, which happens to be among the most expensive.

Nonstick sauté pan: A nonstick sauté pan can be useful for making omelets, and for cooking vegetables and other ingredients without the addition of a lot of fat. Calphalon and All-Clad are two popular brands.

Pots

For making stocks, soups, and braised dishes, a Dutch oven is indispensable. Also useful are pots for reheating sauces, cooking rice, and other smaller jobs. Both All-Clad and Cuisinart make high-quality but pricey pots in an array of shapes and sizes.

Dutch oven: While a Dutch oven is traditionally a large cast-iron pot with a tight-fitting lid and two handles, I normally use a large (8-quart) stainless-steel pot to perform essentially the same tasks.

Small pot: It is a good idea to have a few smaller pots available to prepare any side dishes that will be served with your main meal.

Sachet

A sachet is a mixture of whole spices and herbs such as black peppercorns, bay leaf, thyme, and parsley stems, wrapped in cheesecloth and tied with a string. A sachet imparts flavor to stocks, soups, and sauces while preventing unwanted particles such as stems and leaves from ending up in the final dish. Normally a sachet is placed in the liquid at the beginning of the cooking process, then removed and discarded before serving.

Chapter **2**

The Basics

This chapter explains in detail some of the basic ingredients used throughout the book. You are probably already familiar with many of them, but a few—such as starchless pastas and grapeseed oil—are more obscure and difficult to come across. But with the magic of the Internet, even the most novel ingredients are readily accessible. So take a chance and try something new!

Clarified Butter

Clarified (or drawn) butter is typically made by slowly melting unsalted butter in a pot. The clarified butter is what is left over after the milk solids settle to the bottom of the pot and the white foam that forms on top is scooped away. The major advantage of clarified butter is its higher smoking point (meaning it will not burn as easily), but there will be some loss of flavor. Clarified butter can also be easily made in the microwave: Cut up one stick of unsalted butter, place in a large measuring cup, and microwave uncovered on high for approximately 2 minutes. Use a spoon to scoop away and discard the white foam on top.

The remaining clear yellow liquid is the clarified butter (the milk solids will settle to the bottom). *Ghee,* which is clarified butter that has been simmered until the milk solids turn brown (making it more flavorful), can be purchased in some gourmet markets, health food stores, or on-line.

Crème Fraîche

I discovered crème fraîche while cooking in a French restaurant. It is made from cow's milk, with a flavor and consistency not unlike sour cream. It has become more popular in the United States in recent years, with companies such as Vermont Butter & Cheese Company (www.vtbutterandcheeseco.com) now producing and selling it domestically. Crème fraîche is not a low-fat product, but a little goes a long way. Regular or low-fat sour cream is a good substitute for crème fraîche in most recipes.

Fresh Herbs

The addition of fresh herbs will provide a boost of flavor to everything from soups and sauces to vegetables, pasta, fish, and meat. Different herbs work well with different ingredients, but some classic combinations include tomato and basil, pork and rosemary, and cucumber with dill. I include basil, chervil, chives, cilantro, flat-leaf parsley, mint, rosemary, tarragon, and thyme in recipes throughout this book. Feel free to experiment and find the types and combinations you like the best.

Dried herbs can be substituted in some cases, but for the most part I recommend sticking to fresh whenever possible. Since dried herbs have a stronger flavor than fresh, use approximately half as much dried as fresh in a recipe.

When purchasing fresh herbs, check to make sure that none of the leaves are beginning to turn brown or wilt; they should appear fresh and vibrant, as if still on the plant. Fresh herbs will last as long as a week if stored properly: Wrap them in a slightly damp paper towel and place inside an airtight plastic bag or Tupperware container in the refrigerator.

Many of the recipes in this cookbook call for herbs to be "picked," or removed from their stems. Unless otherwise noted, the leaves are then used in the dish and the stems are discarded.

Gelatin

Thickening liquids using gelatin is a popular method for making desserts, including the Cuisson of Honeydew Melon with Watermelon Gelée in this book (page 163). Gelatin sheets are popular in European cooking, but gelatin powder is more readily available in the United States. The general formula is 1 tablespoon of powdered gelatin equals 4 gelatin leaves.

Before gelatin sheets can be used, they must first be "bloomed": place them in a small cup of cold water and soak to soften, approximately 15 minutes. If using gelatin powder, it must also be soaked first in cold water (follow the packet directions).

Kosher Salt

I like the flavor and coarse texture of kosher salt better than table salt, and I use it throughout this book, as well as at my restaurant. Sea salt also tastes great, but it is normally more expensive than either kosher salt or table salt.

Oils

Many type 2 diabetics, including myself, benefit from a moderate amount of fat in their diet, which can help stabilize blood sugar levels. It is important to consume the right kinds, however—avoid saturated fats, found in red meat, eggs, and dairy products such as cream, as well as the trans-fatty acids in many snack foods. Instead, choose healthy monounsaturated fats such as canola oil, olive oil, grapeseed oil, and nut oils.

Canola oil: Canola oil is high in monounsaturated fat, which researchers believe may have numerous health benefits when used in moderation. In addition, it contains omega-3 fatty acids (also found in fatty fish such as salmon and tuna) that have been linked to lower blood pressure and an increase in HDL or "good" cholesterol levels.

Extra-virgin olive oil: I love the fruity, intense flavor of extra-virgin olive oil, and I use it more often in my cooking than any other fat. Like canola oil, olive oil is high in monounsaturated fat.

Grapeseed oil: Canola and grapeseed oils have similar levels of monounsaturated fat, but I often prefer grapeseed oil in salads, purees, and other dishes because of its light, clean flavor. But grapeseed oil is expensive and often hard to find outside of gourmet food stores or on-line; canola oil may be used instead.

Light olive oil: The newly popular light olive oil can be substituted for extra-virgin olive oil, but there will be a distinct loss of flavor. Light olive oil actually contains the same amount of calories as extra-virgin, so for lightly sautéing foods I definitely recommend sticking with extra-virgin olive oil.

Nut oils: I use nut oils such as walnut oil, hazelnut oil, and pistachio oil in a number of dishes at my restaurant, Trinity. Their distinctive nutty flavor enhances vinaigrettes and purees.

Peppercorns

Store-bought ground pepper doesn't come close to matching the flavor and potency of freshly milled peppercorns. I recommend purchasing two peppermills—one for white peppercorns and another for black.

Black peppercorns: I like to use black pepper when seasoning stronger-flavored ingredients such as steak, lamb, and mushrooms.

White peppercorns: For a milder item such as fish, or if the appearance of black specks in your food is undesired (such as when entertaining guests), white pepper may be preferable.

Spices

Spices are normally dried and include the seeds, berries, and buds of plants. Previously ground spices should be purchased in small quantities and used in a short amount of time, as they tend to lose their flavor quickly. Whole spices last as long as six months in an airtight container in a cool, dark place; after that, they can develop a bitter flavor. Among the spices I use in this book are cumin, nutmeg, peppercorns, and cinnamon.

Starchless Pasta

While most diabetics crave starches just as much—if not more—than everyone else, some types of starch can wreak havoc on your blood sugar levels. Pasta is a refined carbohydrate and should be eaten only in small amounts (you can forget about those all-you-can-eat pasta dinners at Olive Garden). One possible solution is to substitute "starchless" pastas such as lentil linguini, amaranth pasta, and quinoa pasta. These and other starchless pastas are higher in protein than regular pasta; most importantly, they are loaded with fiber because they are complex—not refined—carbohydrates. They can be found in health food stores and online from a variety of sources.

Vinegars

There are numerous vinegars on the market today, including Champagne, cider, rice wine, and herb. The ones I use most often in this book are balsamic, red wine, sherry, and white wine vinegar, all of which have their own distinctive flavors and uses.

Balsamic vinegar: This Italian wine vinegar is traditionally made by aging red wine in wooden barrels. While it is possible to find balsamic vinegars aged twenty-five years or more, these are very expensive and normally used only to drizzle over a finished dish. Commercially produced balsamic vinegars are fine for vinaigrettes and sauces, but balsamic vinegar does contain a high amount of residual sugar and should be used sparingly.

Red wine vinegar: Red wine vinegar is a staple of many home kitchens. It has a stronger flavor than white wine vinegar.

Sherry vinegar: This vinegar is popular in Spanish cooking. It retains the full-bodied flavor of sherry and pairs well with hearty ingredients such as beef, pork, and mushrooms.

White wine vinegar: White wine vinegar has a milder flavor than red wine vinegar and is often cooked with poultry or used to make vinaigrettes.

Chapter 3

Salads

S alads consist of lettuce or other leafy vegetables, often tossed with raw or cooked vegetables, cheese, meat, or nuts, and mixed with a dressing or vinaigrette. The resulting creation can be anything from a simple side salad to an elaborate meal with a multitude of ingredients (such as Grilled Lamb Tenderloin Salad, page 36).

Salads can be found all over the world, often in forms and combinations that you might not recognize. Some omit lettuce altogether, such as an Israeli salad with chopped cucumber, tomato, green pepper, onion, and fresh parsley. However, a salad should always include vegetables, which provide plenty of vitamins and minerals, and almost no calories or fat.

Preparation

Most salad greens have sand or dirt in them, and sometimes even insects, and therefore should be washed well before using. The best method is to first cut the greens into bite-size pieces and then add them to a large bowl or sink filled with cold water, stirring around to wash (do not soak the greens or they will become soggy). After washing, the greens should be dried to help keep them crisp; I suggest purchasing an inexpensive salad spinner, which does the job easily and efficiently.

The basic ingredients in vinaigrettes are oil, vinegar, salt, and pepper. I like to use monounsaturated oils, particularly olive, canola, and grapeseed; polyunsaturated fats such as corn, sunflower, and safflower oils are nutritionally less desirable. There are a multitude of vinegars on the market today, and depending on which type you use, the flavor of the salad can change dramatically. The vinegars used most often in my recipes are red wine, white wine, sherry, and balsamic vinegars.

Healthy Eating

When making a dressing or vinaigrette (or any other food), it is important to measure the number of calories. While salads do contain healthful ingredients such as vegetables, fruit, and nuts, it is still possible to gain weight from eating them. In particular, creamy dressings that are made with fatty ingredients such as regular mayonnaise and sour cream can be especially high in calories. Commercial dressings sold in supermarkets list the amount of total fat, saturated fat, cholesterol, and calories per serving. Low-fat and nonfat commercial dressings are also readily available.

Not surprisingly, the amount of dressing used in a salad will help determine the number of total calories. There should be just enough vinaigrette or dressing to barely cling to the greens and other ingredients in the salad. If you're eating out, one way to ensure that your salad will not be overdressed is to ask for the vinaigrette or dressing on the side and use only a small amount.

Eating salads outside of the house can be a caloric land mine, especially when you do not know exactly what ingredients are in a dressing or vinaigrette. For example, the Crispy Chicken California Cobb Salad at McDonald's has 380 calories and 23 grams of fat; with dressing, tack on another 120 calories and 9 grams of fat (for a total of 500 calories and 31 grams of fat)! Most casual eatery chains and fast food restaurants are now required to make their nutritional information publicly available, so do not be afraid to ask.

Many commercial vinaigrettes and dressings contain a number of preservatives and other additives, but a quick and easy solution is to make your own vinaigrettes, like the ones in this chapter, and use them repeatedly throughout the week. Most dressings and vinaigrettes can be left in the refrigerator for up to 1 week. However, vinaigrettes will separate almost immediately after being made, so be sure to whisk them thoroughly before adding to a salad.

Keep It Exciting

In addition to finding different flavors that work well together, I also focus on colors and textures when creating a salad. For example, my Modern Greek Salad (page 25) attractively combines a number of vegetables, including crisp cucumbers, juicy red and yellow tomatoes, and tender mesclun greens.

Salads are dishes that practically cry out for creativity. Stocking your refrigerator and pantry with a variety of interesting ingredients is a great way to make sure you are able to enjoy a nutritious and exciting salad at home.

The Basic Salad

White balsamic vinegar is made from white wine, and the resulting flavor is lighter and less sweet than traditional balsamic vinegar made with red wine. White balsamic vinegar is available at many supermarkets, but white or red wine vinegar may be substituted if necessary.

MAKES 6 SERVINGS

½ cup extra-virgin olive oil
3 tablespoons white balsamic vinegar
Kosher salt
Freshly milled white pepper
1 English cucumber, skin on, seeded, medium dice
1 pound mesclun salad greens
1 pint cherry tomatoes
1 pint yellow grape tomatoes or 1 yellow bell pepper, medium dice
1 bunch flat-leaf parsley, picked
1 bunch basil, picked

1. To make the vinaigrette, whisk the olive oil and white balsamic vinegar together in a bowl and season with salt and pepper to taste.
2. Combine the cucumber, mesclun, tomatoes, parsley, and basil in a bowl and toss with the vinaigrette.

Variation: Vinaigrettes made with other oils and vinegars can be prepared using the same method as above; for example, balsamic vinegar goes well with a mix of olive oil and canola oil. Experiment with different oils and vinegars until you find what you like best.

Modern Greek Salad

The main elements of a classic Greek salad are lettuce, cucumber, tomato, feta, and olives. In this recipe, I use such modern ingredients as mesclun greens, grape tomatoes, and haricots verts.

MAKES 6 SERVINGS

¾ cup extra-virgin olive oil
¼ cup Chianti vinegar (see note)
Kosher salt
Freshly milled white pepper
½ cup haricots verts
1 pound mesclun salad greens
1 English cucumber, skin on, seeded, medium dice
1 pint cherry tomatoes
1 pint yellow grape tomatoes
1 red onion, sliced thin
1 bunch flat-leaf parsley, picked
1 bunch mint, picked
½ cup Kalamata olives, pitted
½ cup feta cheese, cubed

1. To make the vinaigrette, whisk the olive oil and Chianti vinegar together in a bowl and season with salt and pepper to taste.
2. Blanch and shock the haricots verts. Combine the mesclun, cucumber, tomatoes, onion, parsley, mint, olives, haricots verts, and feta cheese in a bowl and toss with the vinaigrette.

Note: Chianti vinegar is red wine vinegar made from the Chianti grape. Any red wine vinegar will do for this recipe.

Variation: Haricots verts is literally French for "green beans," but in the United States the name normally refers to a specific variety that is tender, thin, and usually more expensive than its domestic counterparts. An equal amount of string beans may be used in place of haricots verts for this recipe.

Caesar Salad with Italian Bread Croutons

I like to present my Caesar salad with whole toasted pieces of bread, rather than cut-up croutons. Not only do I find the presentation to be more elegant, but it is also much easier to control the number of carbohydrates per serving.

MAKES 6 SERVINGS

¼ cup Hellmann's Light Mayonnaise
3 garlic cloves
2 tablespoons red wine vinegar
1 teaspoon Tabasco
1 tablespoon Worcestershire sauce
½ teaspoon fresh lemon juice
2 tablespoons grated Parmesan, plus 2 tablespoons shaved Parmesan
¼ cup extra-virgin olive oil
Kosher salt
Freshly milled white pepper
6 thin slices Italian bread
1 pound romaine lettuce hearts, chopped (6 cups)

1. To make the dressing, combine the mayonnaise, 2 garlic cloves, vinegar, Tabasco, Worcestershire sauce, lemon juice, and grated Parmesan together in a food processor.
2. While the machine is running, slowly drizzle in the olive oil to form a thick dressing. Thin the dressing with a little warm water if necessary and season with salt and pepper to taste. (There will be extra dressing, which can last for up to 2 days in the refrigerator.)
3. For the bread, brush each slice lightly with olive oil. Cut the remaining garlic clove and then rub the bread with the garlic. Toast in an oven or toaster oven until golden brown.
4. Toss the lettuce together with the salad dressing and serve on top of the croutons. Garnish the salad with shaved Parmesan.

Note: When making the salad dressing, be certain to pour in the oil very slowly, or the dressing will "break" and the ingredients will separate, resulting in a thin, watery dressing that both looks and tastes unappealing.

Note: I find it difficult to tell the difference between regular and light Hellmann's Mayonnaise, and by using light mayonnaise for this dressing, the fat and calorie count is cut way back.

Mizuna and Arugula Salad

Mizuna is similar to tatsoi (see page 30) and almost as difficult to find. But no worries, because this salad can be made exclusively with baby arugula, which goes superbly with a soft, creamy goat cheese such as Coach Farm.

MAKES 4 SERVINGS

2 tablespoons Banyuls vinegar (see note)
½ cup extra-virgin olive oil
½ cup grapeseed oil
1 cup mizuna
1 cup baby arugula
Kosher salt
Freshly milled white pepper
½ cup crumbled Coach Farm or other soft goat cheese
¼ cup muscat or white seedless grapes

To make the vinaigrette, whisk the Banyuls vinegar together with the olive oil and grapeseed oil. Toss the mizuna and arugula with the vinaigrette and add salt and pepper to taste just before serving. Garnish with the goat cheese and grapes.

Note: Banyuls is a delightfully sweet French vinegar available online, as well as on the shelves of some gourmet food stores. Sherry or balsamic vinegar may be substituted for Banyuls in this recipe.

Variation: In place of the goat cheese, add grilled squid (see method on page 73) to create a light, refreshing summer salad with less fat and calories and plenty of protein.

Arugula with Walnuts, Blue Cheese, and Asian Pears

The combination of walnuts, blue cheese, and pears with lettuce is a classic French bistro dish. For this salad I chose arugula, because it has more vitamins and minerals than iceberg lettuce and other lighter-colored salad greens. Asian pears are crisp and not too sweet, but almost any kind of apple or pear will do.

MAKES 4 SERVINGS

2 tablespoons red wine vinegar
1 tablespoon sherry vinegar
¼ cup grapeseed oil or canola oil
Kosher salt
Freshly milled black pepper
2 cups baby arugula
½ cup Maytag blue or other blue cheese (see note)
½ cup walnuts, toasted
1 Asian pear, sliced

Whisk together the vinegars, oil, salt, and pepper to make a vinaigrette. Combine the arugula with the blue cheese, walnuts, and Asian pear slices in a salad bowl and toss together with the vinaigrette. Serve in the salad bowl or arrange on individual plates and top with a few slices of the Asian pear for garnish.

Note: Maytag blue cheese comes from Iowa and is widely considered to be one of America's best cheeses. If unavailable, Roquefort or another similarly sharp and strongly flavored blue cheese can be substituted in this recipe.

Salad of Tatsoi and Radishes with Orange-Mustard Vinaigrette

Tatsoi are small, dark green leaves popular in Asian cooking, but they are often unavailable even in gourmet food markets. You can substitute several greens for this salad, including baby spinach, baby arugula, or mizuna.

MAKES 4 SERVINGS

1 tablespoon dry mustard
2 tablespoons Dijon mustard
1 tablespoon brown mustard seed
1 tablespoon yellow mustard seed
¼ cup red wine vinegar
½ cup extra-virgin olive oil
½ cup grapeseed oil
1 pound baby tatsoi
1 bunch red radishes, sliced thin (1 cup)
¼ cup orange segments (from 1 small orange)
Kosher salt
Freshly milled white pepper

For the vinaigrette, whisk the dry mustard and mustard seeds together with the vinegar, olive oil, and grapeseed oil. Toss the tatsoi and radishes with the orange segments, vinaigrette, and salt and pepper to taste just before serving.

Variation: To turn this salad into an elegant entree, add sea scallops (see method for sautéed scallops on page 78). Warm the vinaigrette before tossing with the salad to lightly wilt the greens, and place four scallops on top of each salad. Spoon a little more vinaigrette over the sautéed scallops and serve.

Mâche with Almond Goat Cheese on a Caraway Tuile

Mâche (also called lamb's lettuce or corn salad) is an underappreciated green with small, delicate leaves and a sweet, nutty flavor. It is most often used in salads and goes well with many different kinds of cheeses, including goat cheese, blue cheese, and Camembert. If unavailable, watercress or Boston lettuce may be used instead.

MAKES 4 SERVINGS

Caraway Tuile
  1 cup all-purpose flour
  1 tablespoon plus 1 teaspoon salt
  3 tablespoons confectioner's sugar
  1¼ cups unsalted butter, diced
  1 cup egg whites (from 8 large eggs)
  2 tablespoons caraway seeds
  Freshly milled black pepper

Mâche Salad
  2 tablespoons Banyuls vinegar or balsamic vinegar
  ¼ cup grapeseed oil
  1 tablespoon almond oil
  4-ounce goat cheese log (½ cup)
  ½ cup almonds, toasted and chopped fine
  1 pound mâche (2 cups)
  Kosher salt
  Freshly milled white pepper

1. For the caraway tuiles, mix together the flour, salt, and sugar. Add the butter until well combined and incorporate the egg whites with a hand mixer.

2. Preheat the oven to 300°F. Using a spatula, spread the batter into 8 circular shapes on a baking sheet lined with parchment paper. Sprinkle the caraway seeds and black pepper on top and bake for 8 to 10 minutes or until golden brown.

3. Take the tuiles out of the oven and form each one into a curved shape around a can. Allow the tuiles to cool and dry before using.

Any remaining tuiles may be kept covered in a dry place (not the refrigerator) for up to two days.

4. For the vinaigrette, whisk together the Banyuls vinegar, grapeseed oil, and almond oil and set aside.

5. Turn the oven up to 350°F. Slice the goat cheese log across into 8 pieces and dust with the chopped almonds. Place each piece of almond-dusted goat cheese on a separate tuile.

6. Toss together the mâche and the vinaigrette, add salt and pepper to taste, and serve alongside the goat cheese and caraway tuile.

Variation: In place of the caraway tuile, store-bought crackers such as a crisp flatbread may be used.

Three-Bean Salad with Ginger-Lemon Vinaigrette

The flavors of spring abound in this light, colorful salad. While it makes a fine first course on its own, you can also serve it as a side dish with a number of fish entrees, including the Grilled Halibut and Buckwheat Salad (page 89).

MAKES 4 SERVINGS

1 cup snow pea pods
1 cup sugar snap peas
1 cup haricots verts
½ cup red cherry tomatoes, halved
½ cup yellow cherry tomatoes, halved
¼ cup snow pea shoots
¼ cup basil leaves
2 tablespoons finely minced ginger
¼ cup fresh lemon juice (from 1 to 2 lemons)
1 tablespoon Champagne vinegar or white wine vinegar (see note)
¼ cup extra-virgin olive oil
1 tablespoon honey
Kosher salt
Freshly milled white pepper

1. Blanch the snow pea pods, sugar snap peas, and haricots verts separately in boiling salted water until only slightly crunchy, 2 to 3 minutes; immediately shock each batch in an ice-water bath when done to stop the cooking process and maintain their bright green color.

2. Remove the beans from the water when cooled and dry them off with paper towels or a clean dish towel. Toss the beans together with the tomatoes and set aside.

3. Gently combine the pea shoots and basil together in a separate bowl and refrigerate until they are ready to use to prevent them from wilting.

4. For the vinaigrette, whisk together the ginger, lemon juice, vinegar, olive oil, and honey and season with salt and pepper to taste.

5. Dress the beans lightly with the vinaigrette, and the basil and shoots even more lightly to maintain their texture and avoid the addition of excess fat (from the oil) in your diet.

Note: The slightly sweet Champagne vinegar is a favorite of many chefs, but white wine vinegar is easier to find and will work just as well for this recipe.

Variation: Whenever possible, I recommend using locally grown vegetables for maximum flavor and freshness. So if any of the ingredients called for in this recipe are not in season, feel free to substitute something that is; for example, you can replace the snow pea shoots with a handful of mesclun greens if necessary.

Haricots verts is literally French for "green beans," but in the United States the name normally refers to a specific variety that is tender, thin, and usually more expensive than its domestic counterparts. An equal amount of string beans may be used in place of haricots verts for this recipe.

Cucumber-Mango Salad

To turn this salad appetizer into a larger meal, serve it with seafood, such as grilled shrimp, soft-shell crabs, or raw oysters.

MAKES 6 SERVINGS

8 beefsteak tomatoes
1 tablespoon red wine vinegar
Kosher salt
Freshly milled white pepper
2 English cucumbers, peeled and seeded, medium dice
1 cup halved cherry tomatoes
1 red onion, small dice
1 mango, peeled, medium dice
½ cup fresh basil, chiffonade
1 tablespoon extra-virgin olive oil

1. Cut the beefsteak tomatoes in half horizontally and place them in a microwave-safe casserole dish. Microwave the tomatoes on high for 4 minutes.
2. Remove the tomatoes and use the back of a large spoon to gently press them through a strainer to make "tomato water."
3. Stir the tomato water together with the vinegar and season with salt and pepper to taste. Set aside until ready to use.
4. In a mixing bowl, combine the cucumbers with the cherry tomatoes, onion, mango, and basil and season with salt and pepper to taste.
5. Place the salad in the center of a large bowl. Pour enough tomato water around the salad to come approximately halfway up the sides. Drizzle the salad lightly with olive oil and serve.

Note: If you do not own a microwave, the beefsteak tomatoes can be prepared using a large sauté pan. Cut the tomatoes in half horizontally and place them cut-side down in the pan in a single layer. Turn the heat on low and cook the tomatoes until they soften and begin to lose their shape, approximately 10 to 15 minutes. Proceed with step 2 above.

Grilled Lamb Tenderloin Salad

The addition of lamb to the Modern Greek Salad (page 25) makes this dish a complete meal, with plenty of protein and other important nutrients. As its name would suggest, the tenderloin is quite tender (think filet mignon) and will cook more quickly than other cuts of meat.

MAKES 6 SERVINGS

2 pounds lamb tenderloin
1 tablespoon extra-virgin olive oil
1 tablespoon chopped rosemary
1 tablespoon chopped thyme
1 garlic clove, crushed
1 shallot, sliced
Kosher salt
Freshly milled black pepper
Modern Greek Salad (page 25)
6 ounces pita chips, optional (see note)

1. Marinate the lamb in the olive oil, rosemary, thyme, garlic, and shallot for 30 minutes in the refrigerator.
2. Remove the lamb from the marinade and season with salt and pepper to taste. Grill on a grill pan or outdoor barbecue until of desired doneness, approximately 3 minutes per side for medium rare and 4 minutes per side for medium.
3. Allow the meat to rest on a cutting board for 10 minutes to redistribute the juices. Cut the meat against the grain into ¼-inch-thick slices.
4. Toss together the lamb and the Modern Greek Salad with the vinaigrette. Serve with the pita chips, if using.

Note: Pita chips are commercially available, but they are also very easy to make. Cut a piece of pita bread (preferably whole wheat) into triangular wedges, brush lightly with olive oil on both sides, and bake in an oven or toaster oven at 400°F until crisp, approximately 10 minutes.

Variation: For a more elegant presentation, place the dressed salad into a shallow bowl, fan the lamb pieces over the top of the salad, and drizzle additional vinaigrette on top of the lamb.

Chapter 4

Stocks, Soups, and Purees

Purees are essentially very thick soups, so to me it makes sense to include them in the same chapter. In fact, most purees—including the Mushroom Puree (page 53) and Carrot-Ginger Puree (page 59)—can be turned into soups simply by adding a flavorful liquid such as vegetable or chicken stock.

Stocks

I think of stocks as building blocks for a great meal. While it may seem like an extra step to make stock (especially when it would be much easier to buy canned broth or bouillon cubes at the supermarket), the results are well worth the effort. Also, you can make stocks ahead of time in large batches—most stocks will keep in the refrigerator for up to 1 week or in the freezer for as long as 2 months. Tip: After making stock, store it in individual pint containers and remove each one as you need it.

Soups

All the soups in this chapter make ideal appetizers or small meals for diabetics. Some are also hearty enough to serve as a main course for lunch or even dinner, such as Grandma's Chicken Soup served with rice or pasta (page 51) or Mushroom Lentil Soup (page 48); they are full of vitamins, protein, and other elements important to the diabetic diet, in addition to being low in fat.

Soups also help you feel full without the addition of a lot of calories, fat, or carbohydrates, so a cup in the middle of the afternoon can help satisfy your food cravings. In fact, eating small snacks in between meals is a great way to control your blood sugar levels, as long as the food you are snacking on is a part of your overall diet plan. Avoid foods that are low in nutritional value and high in carbohydrates, such as cookies, potato chips, and candy, along with high-calorie foods such as french fries and pizza. Your body will thank you for it later.

To help maintain freshness, cool soup down as quickly as possible after it is finished cooking. Fill a kitchen sink approximately halfway with ice water (use plenty of ice) and place the pot of soup in the ice bath to cool; stir occasionally with a large spoon and when cool immediately place it in the refrigerator.

Purees

Diabetics like foods that are both rich and sweet—it is just something we crave. Purees serve to satisfy these cravings and satiate us by enhancing the natural sweetness of vegetables through roasting, as well as offering richness without a lot of fat.

The most important tool for making purees is a good blender, preferably one with variable speeds and a pulse option (Waring and Cuisinart both make good-quality models). To avoid injury when using a blender to puree hot ingredients, it is important to take the following precautions: do not fill the blender more than halfway, do cover and wrap a kitchen towel over the top, and be sure to hold the top down tightly as you blend.

Most purees are simple to prepare and almost impossible to overcook. Nevertheless, I would suggest chopping the vegetables into approximately equal pieces, which ensures that everything is cooked at the same rate (for example, if one piece of carrot is 1 inch long and another is only ¼ inch, the smaller piece will finish cooking first). The goal is to simmer the vegetables until they are soft enough to puree. To check for doneness, use the fork method—if you pierce the vegetables with a fork and it goes through cleanly without anything clinging to it, they are ready to be pureed. Alternatively, use a spoon to press a piece against the side of the pot; if it falls apart, the vegetables are ready to be pureed.

The purees in this chapter go extremely well with a wide variety of meat, fish, and seafood dishes. For a more elegant presentation, spoon several purees side by side on the same plate; for example, halibut can be served together on a plate with dollops of Mushroom Puree (page 53), Carrot-Ginger Puree (page 59), and Artichoke Oreganata Puree (page 62).

Another advantage of purees is they are ideal for making in large batches and saving for later. In general, purees may be stored in the refrigerator for up to 1 week or the freezer for as long as 1 month.

Purees can be easily reheated in a microwave without any loss of flavor. Alternatively, warm them on low heat in a heavy-bottomed pot, stirring often with a spoon to avoid burning.

Some of the puree recipes in this chapter call for using butter, but the amounts are too small to affect your overall calorie count significantly. Butter is a saturated fat, and diets high in saturated fat can contribute to heart disease, a disorder for which diabetics are already at risk. For a healthier puree, use an equal amount of olive oil in place of the butter—olive oil is a monounsaturated fat, which research indicates may lower LDL ("bad") cholesterol and raise the body's level of HDL ("good") cholesterol.

Vegetable Stock

Vegetarian chefs have long known that vegetable stock is a great way to flavor soups and sauces without the addition of any meat products. In addition, it is filled with vitamins and other important nutrients. I actually prefer using vegetable stock over chicken stock when preparing lighter soups and sauces, and I use vegetable stock in the Asparagus Flan and Sautéed Chanterelles recipe in this book (page 144).

MAKES 4 QUARTS

½ bunch flat-leaf parsley
1 thyme sprig
1 bay leaf
15 black peppercorns
2 tablespoons canola oil
5 celery stalks, chopped
1 white onion, chopped
2 carrots, chopped
3 leeks, white parts only, chopped
1 large fennel bulb, chopped
1 garlic head, halved horizontally

1. Make a sachet with the parsley, thyme, bay leaf, and peppercorns. Heat a Dutch oven on low; add the canola oil and sauté the celery, onion, carrots, leeks, and fennel until they begin to soften, approximately 10 minutes. Add 4 quarts of cold water, the garlic, and the sachet, and simmer for 1 hour.
2. Strain and cool down the liquid using an ice bath. This stock can be refrigerated for up to 5 days or frozen in pint containers for up to 2 months.

Variation: Other vegetables that can be used in making this stock include mushrooms, parsnips, turnips, and shallots.

Mushroom Stock

This richly flavored but low-calorie stock can be used in place of beef or chicken stock in any dish that pairs well with mushrooms, including Open-Faced Mushroom "Ravioli" (page 142).

MAKES 1 QUART

2 tablespoons grapeseed oil
1 onion, chopped
2 celery stalks, chopped
1 carrot, chopped
2 garlic cloves, chopped
25 to 30 white button mushrooms, chopped (3 cups)
1 bunch thyme

1. Heat a Dutch oven on medium for 3 minutes. Add the grapeseed oil, onion, celery, and carrots, and cook until the onion becomes translucent, approximately 4 minutes (stir occasionally to keep the vegetables from browning).
2. Add the garlic, mushrooms, and thyme and continue cooking and stirring to soften the vegetables, an additional 15 minutes.
3. Cover the vegetables with 2 quarts of cold water, bring just to a boil, and simmer uncovered for 30 minutes.
4. Turn off the heat and allow the ingredients to sit in the pot for 30 minutes more. Pour the mushroom stock through a fine mesh strainer and discard the solids.

Variation: This stock can be made with just about any mushrooms you have available, although different types will produce different flavors.

Basic Chicken Stock

Chicken stock gives soups, sauces, and other dishes an added boost of flavor when used in place of water. I always prefer fresh chicken stock if it is available, but canned broth is fine as long as the sodium content is not too high. If using canned chicken broth, look for products labeled "low-sodium."

MAKES 4 QUARTS

8 pounds chicken wings
½ bunch flat-leaf parsley
1 bay leaf
2 thyme sprigs
15 black peppercorns
1 small celery root bulb, peeled and large dice
1 carrot, diced
1 onion, quartered
2 garlic cloves

1. Place the chicken wings into a large pot with 4 quarts of cold water. Bring the water just to a boil and then turn it down to a simmer. Skim off any impurities that float to the top.
2. Make a sachet with the parsley, bay leaf, thyme, and peppercorns. Add the celery root, carrot, onion, garlic, and sachet to the pot. Continue simmering for 2 hours, occasionally skimming any impurities and fat that float to the top.
3. Turn off the heat and remove any remaining fat and impurities from the surface with a ladle. Carefully pour out the chicken stock through a colander lined with cheesecloth, being careful not to disturb the solids on the bottom of the pot. Discard the remaining chicken parts and vegetables.
4. Cool down the stock in an ice-water bath and then refrigerate for up to 1 week or freeze in individual pint containers for as long as 2 months.

Note: I do not put salt in my chicken stock, because it can be added at any time when preparing a dish—whatever salt you put in cannot be taken out again, which may be a problem if the stock is being used to make something that requires little or no salt.

Variation: In addition to the vegetables found in this recipe, celery stalks, leeks, and shallots are also commonly used in making chicken stock.

Variation: For a richer-tasting brown stock, first roast the chicken wings and vegetables in a preheated 400°F oven until dark brown (not burnt), approximately 30 to 45 minutes. Then proceed with the recipe as directed above.

Basic Beef Stock

Beef stock is used in place of water to flavor rich and hearty dishes, such as Poached Filet Mignon with Asian Vegetables and Egg Noodles (page 117) and Prime Sirloin Steak with Vidalia Onion Jus (page 119).

MAKES 1 GALLON

10 pounds beef bones (see note)
1 bunch flat-leaf parsley
1 bay leaf
2 thyme sprigs
1 tablespoon black peppercorns
1 small celery root bulb, peeled, large dice
1 carrot, large dice
1 onion, quartered
2 garlic cloves
2 plum tomatoes

1. Rinse the beef bones and put them into a large pot with 4 quarts of cold water. Bring the water just to a boil and then turn down to a simmer. Skim off any impurities that float to the top.
2. Make a sachet with the parsley, bay leaf, thyme, and peppercorns. Add the celery root, carrot, onion, garlic, plum tomatoes and sachet to the pot. Continue simmering for 4 hours, occasionally skimming any impurities and fat that float to the top.
3. Turn off the heat and remove any remaining fat and impurities from the surface with a ladle. Carefully pour out the beef stock through a colander lined with cheesecloth, being careful not to disturb the solids on the bottom of the pot. Discard the beef bones and vegetables.
4. Cool down the stock in an ice-water bath and then refrigerate for up to 1 week or freeze in individual pint containers for as long as 2 months.

Note: You can use a number of different types of beef bones to make this stock, but the best ones are from the back and neck—ask your butcher if they have leftovers to sell you.

Variation: The same technique used here can be employed to make Veal Stock. Simply replace the beef bones with an equal amount of veal bones and continue with the recipe as directed above.

Dashi (Japanese Stock)

Dashi is to Japanese cuisine what chicken stock is to Western cooking. Dashi is used to make miso soup and other broths, as well as the Steamed Mussels Hot Pot (page 68). The main ingredients in dashi are kombu (kelp, a kind of seaweed) and dried bonito flakes (bonito is a type of tuna).

MAKES 2 QUARTS

3 tablespoons kombu, rinsed
1½ tablespoons bonito flakes

1. Bring 2 quarts of water to a boil and then turn down to a simmer. Add the kombu and simmer for 10 minutes.
2. Turn off the heat and add the bonito flakes. Steep for 30 minutes and then strain through a fine mesh strainer. When straining, do not press down on the bonito and kombu or the stock will become cloudy.
3. Cool down the dashi and store in the refrigerator. It will keep for up to 4 days if stored properly.

Variation: Hon dashi crystals can be used in place of dashi. Hon dashi is a dried concentrate made with kombu and bonito flakes, but it often contains monosodium glutamate as well. To prepare, bring 2 cups of cold water and 1½ teaspoons hon dashi to a simmer. Steep off of the heat for at least 5 minutes and then pour the broth through a fine mesh strainer.

Sake Broth

This is an extremely flavorful Japanese broth that enhances the taste of shellfish such as the Steamed Mussels Hot Pot (page 68), as well as delicate fish such as cod and Steamed Bass with Shiitake Mushrooms and Baby Bok Choy (page 85).

MAKES 2½ QUARTS

2 quarts Dashi (page 46)
1 tablespoon grated fresh ginger
1 tablespoon minced garlic
1 cup low-sodium soy sauce
½ cup sake
2 tablespoons sweet cooking rice wine
½ cup scallions, chopped

Slowly bring all of the ingredients to a simmer (be sure not to boil the broth, or it will become cloudy). Simmer for 20 minutes and then remove from the heat. Let the broth steep for another 20 minutes before straining through a piece of cheesecloth. Cool down and store in the refrigerator until ready to use (up to 4 days).

Mushroom Lentil Soup

Cooked French green lentils hold their shape well, making them a good choice for this soup. Brown lentils may be substituted, however, as they are usually easier to find in supermarkets.

MAKES 12 SERVINGS

1 tablespoon grapeseed oil
1 tablespoon chopped onion
2 teaspoons chopped celery
2 teaspoons chopped carrot
2 garlic cloves, chopped
15 to 20 white button mushrooms, chopped (2 cups)
1 cup green or brown lentils (see note)
4 cups chicken stock
1 tablespoon crème fraîche
1 teaspoon kosher salt
½ teaspoon freshly milled black pepper

1. Warm a saucepot on medium heat for approximately 3 minutes. Add the grapeseed oil and then the onion, celery, carrot, and garlic. Cook until the vegetables are tender but not brown, approximately 4 minutes, lowering heat if necessary.
2. Add the mushrooms, lentils, and chicken stock. Cover the pot and simmer until the lentils are tender but not mushy, approximately 30 minutes.
3. Remove half of the mixture from the pot and transfer to a blender. Add the crème fraîche, salt, and pepper, and process until smooth.
4. Combine the smooth and coarse mixtures with a whisk. Taste the mixture and add additional seasoning if necessary.

Note: Before using lentils in a recipe, it is important to rinse them well and check closely for pebbles with your fingers.

Variation: For a heartier, thicker soup, mix in 1 cup of Mushroom Puree (page 53) just before serving.

Variation: In place of lentils, substitute an equal measurement of barley, a good source of soluble fiber, or the same amount of quinoa, which is high in protein.

Cauliflower-Leek Potage

Madras curry powder, a mild and evenly balanced mix of spices, gives this thick, creamy soup its distinctive flavor; any commercial curry powder may be used, however. Curries include a number of ingredients such as curry leaves, turmeric, coriander, cumin, chile pepper, clove, black pepper, and other spices.

MAKES 8 SERVINGS

2 heads cauliflower
2 garlic cloves, chopped
4 leeks, white parts only, cleaned and chopped
½ cup crème fraîche
1 tablespoon clarified butter
1 teaspoon Madras curry powder
1 teaspoon kosher salt
½ teaspoon freshly milled white pepper

1. Cut off the thick stem of the cauliflower and discard. Separate the cauliflower heads into individual florets with your hands or a knife and rinse under cold water to clean.
2. Combine the cauliflower, garlic, and leeks and add 4 cups of water. Bring to a boil, then turn down to a simmer. Cover the pot and cook the vegetables until fork tender, approximately 30 minutes.
3. Drain the vegetables, reserving the liquid for later use. Add the vegetables to a blender along with the crème fraîche and process until smooth.
4. Heat a sauté pan on medium to melt the clarified butter and add the Madras curry. Continue stirring the curry butter around in the pan for 2 to 3 minutes, then pass it through a fine mesh strainer. Add the curry butter to the puree.
5. Add the reserved liquid as needed until the desired thickness is achieved. Season with salt and pepper.

Pumpkin-Pie-Spiced Carrot Soup

The cinnamon and allspice in this recipe give the soup a distinctive flavor. Allspice is a common ingredient in Caribbean cooking (as well as in pumpkin pie), with a flavor somewhat similar to cloves.

MAKES 16 SERVINGS

20 carrots, diced
2 white onions, diced
3 tablespoons sliced peeled ginger
1 garlic clove, chopped
4 tablespoons unsalted butter
2 bay leaves
1 teaspoon allspice
2 cinnamon sticks
½ cup fresh orange juice (from 3 to 4 oranges) (see note)
1 teaspoon kosher salt
½ teaspoon freshly milled white pepper

1. Combine the carrots, onion, ginger, and garlic with the butter in a Dutch oven and sauté lightly on medium heat until the onions are translucent, approximately 5 minutes.
2. Make a sachet with the bay leaves, allspice, and cinnamon sticks. Add 2 quarts of water and the orange juice and bring to a boil. Turn the heat down to a simmer and add the sachet. Cover the pot and cook until the carrots are fork tender, approximately 45 minutes. Discard the sachet.
3. Add the ingredients to a blender and process until smooth. Season with salt and pepper. Add more liquid and seasoning if needed to achieve the desired consistency and taste.

Note: Valencia oranges are excellent for juicing and often less expensive than other varieties. If you don't feel like making your own, fresh orange juice purchased from a store is fine for this recipe; just make sure to check the sell-by date.

Grandma's Chicken Soup

My grandmother and mother made this soup for me when I was growing up in Brooklyn, but with a few changes it can become any grandma's soup— use Asian touches such as lemongrass and cilantro leaves, add spicy chiles to give it a Mexican flair, or include different root vegetables such as turnips and rutabaga . . . the possibilities are endless!

MAKES 16 SERVINGS

1 bunch parsley stems
15 whole black peppercorns
1 whole chicken (4 pounds) (see note)
1 small celery root bulb, peeled and medium dice (½ cup)
1 carrot, medium dice
½ onion, medium dice
1 parsnip, peeled and medium dice
2 garlic cloves, minced
2 tablespoons kosher salt
1 bunch dill, picked

1. Wrap the parsley stems and peppercorns in a sachet. Rinse the chicken and discard the skin and innards. Cut into pieces (legs, thighs, breasts, and wings) and place in a large pot with 4 quarts of water, the sachet, celery root, carrots, onion, parsnip, and garlic.

2. Bring the soup to a boil and then reduce to a simmer. Cover the pot and continue to cook for 1 hour, occasionally skimming off any impurities and fat from the surface.

3. Remove the chicken and allow it to cool enough to handle. Remove all the bones and cartilage and pull apart the meat into bite-size pieces.

4. Discard the sachet and season the soup with salt. Add the chicken back to the pot and cool uncovered in an ice bath. Remove any fat that has congealed on top with a spoon. Return the soup to a simmer and add the dill just before serving.

Note: I like to use organic chicken when available, but any kind will do for this soup as long as it is fresh and comes from a reputable source.

Variation: To turn this soup into a meal, add 2 ounces of cooked rice (preferably brown) or al dente pasta (such as whole-wheat noodles) per portion. To avoid overcooking, prepare the rice or pasta separately and add to the soup just before serving.

Variation: Fresh chicken stock may be used in place of water in this recipe for a more full-flavored soup.

Mushroom Puree

This basic puree is extremely versatile and can be served with a wide variety of dishes, including Pan-Seared Monkfish with (Not Your Mother's) Peas and Carrots (page 95), Chicken Paillard with Avocado-Tomatillo Salsa and Quinoa Pilaf (page 105), and Pan-Roasted Filet Mignon with Sautéed Mustard Greens (page 115).

MAKES 1 QUART

1 tablespoon grapeseed oil
1 tablespoon diced onion
2 teaspoons celery, medium dice
2 teaspoons carrots, medium dice
2 garlic cloves, chopped
15 to 20 white button mushrooms, chopped (2 cups)
½ cup chicken stock
1 tablespoon crème fraîche, sour cream, or low-fat sour cream
1 teaspoon kosher salt
½ teaspoon freshly milled black pepper

1. Warm a sauté pan on medium heat for approximately 3 minutes. Add the grapeseed oil, followed by the onion, celery, carrots, and garlic. Cook until tender but not brown, approximately 4 minutes (lowering heat if necessary).
2. Add the mushrooms and cook at medium-high heat until all the liquid in the pan has evaporated, approximately 5 minutes.
3. Pour in the chicken stock and simmer until the liquid is evaporated and the mixture is once again dry, about 5 more minutes.
4. Remove the mixture from the pan and transfer to a blender. Add the crème fraîche, salt, and pepper and process until smooth. Taste the puree and add additional seasoning if necessary.

Variation: For a more flavorful and exciting puree, use exotic mushrooms such as shiitake (stems removed), chanterelle, or porcini, either by themselves or in combination. And for an even deeper, more complex taste, sauté the mushrooms until browned.

Celery Root Puree

This puree will go well with most dishes that can be served with mashed potatoes, including Prime Sirloin Steak with Vidalia Onion Jus (page 119). It is also much healthier for diabetics than potatoes, because the carbohydrate count in celery root is far lower.

MAKES 1 QUART

> 2 medium celery root bulbs, peeled and large dice
> 1 cup milk
> ¼ cup fresh lemon juice (from 1 to 2 lemons)
> ¼ cup crème fraîche, sour cream, or low-fat sour cream (see note)
> 1 teaspoon kosher salt
> ½ teaspoon freshly milled white pepper

1. Add the celery root, milk, lemon juice, and 2 cups of water to a Dutch oven. Bring the ingredients to a boil, then turn the heat down to a simmer and cook until the vegetables are fork tender, approximately 30 minutes.
2. Preheat the oven to 350°F. Drain the celery root, place on a baking sheet, and cook in the oven until it begins to dry out, approximately 10 minutes.
3. Add the celery root to a blender along with the crème fraîche and process until smooth. Season with salt and pepper.

Note: To reduce the amount of fat in this puree, substitute the milk with an equal amount of 1% or 2% milk. Even skim milk will work, but the resulting puree will taste less rich.

Parsnip–Celery Root Puree

Serve this puree with heartier meats such as venison and other game meats, or try it with the Pan-Roasted Filet Mignon with Sautéed Mustard Greens (page 115).

MAKES 1 QUART

3 parsnips, peeled and large dice
1 medium celery root bulb, peeled and large dice
1 cup milk or low-fat milk
¼ cup fresh lemon juice (from 1 to 2 lemons)
¼ cup crème fraîche
1 teaspoon kosher salt
½ teaspoon freshly milled white pepper

1. Combine the parsnip and celery root with the milk, lemon juice, and 2 cups of water in a Dutch oven and bring the ingredients to a boil. Turn down to a simmer and cook the vegetables until fork tender, approximately 40 minutes.
2. Preheat the oven to 350°F. Drain the vegetables and cook on a baking sheet in the oven until they begin to dry out, approximately 10 minutes.
3. Place the parsnips and celery root in a blender along with the crème fraîche and process until smooth. Season with salt and pepper.

Truffle-Pea Puree

Truffles in all their forms (white, black, summer, and winter) are becoming increasingly popular in America's top restaurants, but the cost remains prohibitive for most home cooks. Truffle oil and truffle butter are two products that capture the flavor of truffles without breaking the bank; both can be found in many gourmet food stores and on a number of food websites.

MAKES 1 QUART

1 tablespoon unsalted butter
2 tablespoons shallots, chopped
¼ cup white wine
½ cup chicken stock
Three 10-ounce boxes frozen peas
1 tablespoon black truffle oil
3 tablespoons crème fraîche
1 teaspoon kosher salt
½ teaspoon freshly milled black pepper
2 tablespoons black truffle butter

1. Warm a saucepot on medium heat for 3 minutes. Add the butter and then the shallots. Cook the shallots until tender but not brown, approximately 10 minutes (lowering heat if necessary).
2. Deglaze with white wine and cook until all the liquid in the pan has evaporated, an additional 5 minutes.
3. Add the chicken stock and peas and simmer until the peas are hot, approximately 5 minutes.
4. Remove the mixture from the pot and transfer to a blender. Add the truffle oil, crème fraîche, salt, and pepper, and process until smooth. Add the truffle butter and pulse to incorporate. Taste the mixture and add additional seasoning if necessary.

Truffle–Celery Root Puree

Celery root (or celeriac) is one of my favorite vegetables. It has an earthy, celery-like flavor, with the heartiness of a root vegetable. Truffle mashed potatoes is a classic combination, so to me this dish makes perfect sense.

MAKES 1 QUART

2 medium celery root bulbs, peeled and large dice
1 cup milk or low-fat milk
¼ cup fresh lemon juice (from 1 to 2 lemons)
¼ cup crème fraîche
¼ cup black truffle butter
1 teaspoon kosher salt
½ teaspoon freshly milled white pepper

1. Combine the celery root with the milk, lemon juice, and 2 cups of water and bring to a boil. Turn down to a simmer and cook until the vegetables are fork tender, approximately 30 minutes.

2. Preheat an oven to 350°F. Drain the celery root and cook on a baking sheet in the oven until it begins to dry out, approximately 10 minutes.

3. Add the celery root to a blender along with the crème fraîche and truffle butter and process until smooth. Season with salt and pepper.

Truffle-Leek Puree

Leeks are usually filled with dirt or sand, so they should be thoroughly cleaned before using. Slice the leek in half lengthwise and rinse well under cold running water, using your fingers to separate the layers and remove any remaining particles.

MAKES 1 QUART

1 tablespoon grapeseed oil
5 to 6 leeks, white parts only, washed and chopped (3 cups)
¼ cup white wine
½ cup chicken stock
1 tablespoon black truffle oil
2 tablespoons crème fraîche
1 teaspoon kosher salt
½ teaspoon freshly milled black pepper
2 tablespoons black truffle butter

1. Warm a sauté pan on medium heat for approximately 3 minutes. Add the grapeseed oil and then the leeks. Cook the leeks until tender but not brown, approximately 15 minutes, lowering the heat if necessary.
2. Add the white wine and bring to a simmer. Cook until the mixture is dry, an additional 10 minutes.
3. Add the chicken stock and simmer until all of the liquid is evaporated and the mixture is once again dry, approximately 5 minutes.
4. Remove the leeks from the pan and transfer to a blender. Add the truffle oil, crème fraîche, salt, and pepper and process until smooth. Add the truffle butter and pulse to incorporate the ingredients. Taste the puree and add additional seasoning if necessary.

Carrot-Ginger Puree

If you don't love the flavor of ginger, reduce the amount or even cut it out altogether; just replace the ginger with an extra garlic clove at the beginning of the cooking process.

MAKES 1 QUART

2 to 3 carrots, diced (2 cups)
1 tablespoon peeled and sliced ginger
1 garlic clove, chopped
4 tablespoons unsalted butter
¼ cup crème fraîche
1 teaspoon kosher salt
½ teaspoon freshly milled white pepper

1. Add the carrots, ginger, and garlic to a Dutch oven along with the butter and sauté the ingredients lightly until they begin to soften but not brown, approximately 5 minutes.
2. Add 2 cups of water, bring to a boil, and then lower to a simmer. Cook the carrots until fork tender, approximately 40 minutes. Drain the carrots over a bowl, reserving the liquid for later use.
3. Add the carrots to a blender along with the crème fraîche and process until smooth. Season with salt and pepper. Add the reserved liquid as needed, until the desired consistency is achieved.

Sunchoke Puree

The sunchoke (Jerusalem artichoke) is a root vegetable with a sweet, nutty flavor. Sunchokes are often hard to find outside of greenmarkets or specialty grocers; three or four parsnips may be substituted in this dish if necessary.

MAKES 1 QUART

1 tablespoon grapeseed oil
1 tablespoon chopped onion
2 teaspoons chopped celery
2 teaspoons chopped carrot
15 to 20 sunchokes, peeled and sliced (2 cups)
¼ cup white wine
½ cup chicken stock
1 tablespoon sherry vinegar
1 tablespoon crème fraîche
1 teaspoon kosher salt
½ teaspoon freshly milled black pepper

1. Warm a sauté pan on medium heat for 3 minutes. Add the grapeseed oil and then the onion, celery, and carrots. Cook until tender but not brown, approximately 4 minutes (lowering heat if necessary).
2. Add the sunchokes and cook on medium heat until the vegetables are caramelized, approximately 10 minutes.
3. Add the white wine, bring to a simmer, and cook until the liquid is evaporated, around 5 minutes.
4. Add chicken stock and simmer until all the liquid is evaporated and the mixture is once again dry, around 10 more minutes.
5. Remove the mixture from the pan and transfer to a blender. Add the vinegar, crème fraîche, salt, and pepper and process until smooth. Taste and add additional seasoning if necessary.

Cauliflower-Almond Puree

A key ingredient in this recipe is almond oil, available at most gourmet retailers and some online food sites. Nut oils including almond, walnut, hazelnut, and pistachio are monounsaturated, helping raise desired HDL cholesterol and lower "bad" LDL cholesterol . . . and they taste great too.

MAKES 1 QUART

2 heads cauliflower
1 garlic clove, chopped
1 leek, white part only, cleaned and chopped
4 tablespoons unsalted butter
½ cup almonds, toasted (see note)
2 tablespoons almond oil
¼ cup crème fraîche
1 teaspoon kosher salt
½ teaspoon freshly milled white pepper

1. Cut off the thick stem from the cauliflower and discard. Separate the cauliflower heads into individual florets with your hands or a knife and rinse under cold water to clean.
2. Place the cauliflower, garlic, leeks, and butter in a Dutch oven and add 2 cups of water. Bring to a boil and then turn down to a simmer. Cook vegetables until fork tender, about 30 minutes. Drain the vegetables over a bowl, reserving the liquid for later use.
3. Add the vegetables to a blender, along with the toasted almonds, almond oil, and crème fraîche, and process until smooth. Season with salt and pepper and adjust the consistency using the reserved liquid until the desired consistency is achieved.

Note: To toast almonds or almost any dried nuts, place them on a baking sheet in an oven or toaster oven in a single layer and cook at 350°F until golden brown, approximately 10 minutes. Shake the tray periodically to avoid uneven cooking, and check the nuts often to make sure they do not burn.

Alternatively, you can cook the almonds in a dry sauté pan on medium heat, tossing them every minute or so to ensure even browning.

Artichoke Oreganata Puree

Artichokes and bread crumbs give this puree an Italian twist. Although the recipe calls for fresh artichoke bottoms, they can be replaced with an equal amount of frozen artichoke hearts.

MAKES 1 QUART

2 tablespoons unsalted butter

1 tablespoon chopped onion

2 teaspoons chopped celery

2 teaspoons chopped carrot

2 garlic cloves, chopped

2 cups fresh artichoke bottoms (4 to 6 artichokes), or 2 cups frozen artichoke hearts

2 lemons

¼ cup white wine

½ cup chicken stock

1 tablespoon white wine vinegar

1 tablespoon sour cream or low-fat sour cream

1 teaspoon kosher salt

½ teaspoon freshly milled black pepper

¼ cup dried Italian-seasoned bread crumbs

1. Warm a sauté pan on medium heat for approximately 3 minutes. Add the butter and then the onion, celery, carrot, and garlic. Cook until tender but not brown, about 10 minutes, lowering the heat if necessary.
2. To prepare fresh artichoke bottoms (if using), follow these steps:
   a. To prevent the artichokes from browning, fill a bowl with cold water and squeeze the juice from the lemons into the bowl. Prepare the artichoke bottoms one at a time, placing each one in the lemon water as soon as they are trimmed.
   b. Cut off the stem of the artichoke, followed by the top of the leaves above the heart.
   c. Snap off the outer leaves and use a paring knife to remove the remaining leaves.
   d. Cut the artichoke bottom in half. Scoop out the hairy inner choke with a small spoon and discard.

3. Add the fresh artichoke bottoms to the pan, if using, and continue cooking until completely tender, approximately 10 minutes more. If using frozen artichoke hearts, add them to the pan at this point and cook until hot, approximately 5 minutes.
4. Deglaze with white wine. Add chicken stock and simmer until most of the liquid in the pan has evaporated, around 5 minutes. Remove the mixture from the pan and transfer to a blender.
5. Add the vinegar, sour cream, salt, and pepper and blend until smooth. Add the bread crumbs and process until incorporated. Taste the puree and add additional seasoning if necessary.

Chapter 5

Seafood

S eafood is high in protein, low in fat, and full of essential vitamins and minerals, making it an ideal component of any healthy diabetic diet.

Healthy Protein

Firm white fish such as cod and halibut are particularly healthful for diabetics compared to most animal proteins, because they are high in protein and low in fat. For example, 3 ounces of skinless black sea bass contain approximately 100 calories, 20 grams of protein, 2 grams of fat, and only 40 milligrams of cholesterol. Comparatively, a 3-ounce piece of sirloin steak has about 240 calories, 23 grams of protein, 15 grams of fat, and 77 milligrams of cholesterol.

Shrimp and some other shellfish are relatively high in cholesterol; however, they are also good sources of protein and contain almost no saturated fat, making them a perfectly acceptable part of a diabetic diet when consumed in moderation. Other shellfish, including scallops, squid, and clams, are low in cholesterol in addition to being high in protein and low in fat. Three ounces of shrimp contain about 100 calories, 21 grams of protein, 1 gram of fat, and 130 milligrams of cholesterol, versus 75 calories, 15 grams of protein, less than 1 gram of fat, and only 30 milligrams of cholesterol for three large scallops.

Omega-3 Fatty Acids

According to the American Diabetes Association, people with diabetes have a greater risk of heart disease earlier in life. One way to combat this trend is to consume omega-3 fatty acids, which are found in many fatty fish, including salmon, tuna, mackerel, and bluefish. Omega-3 has been linked to an increase in "good" HDL cholesterol levels and a decrease in "bad" LDL cholesterol, as well as lower blood pressure, the prevention of blood clots, and healthy brain development.

The American Heart Association confirms that omega-3 fatty acids contribute to heart health in both healthy people and those at high risk of cardiovascular disease. As a result, their nutrition guidelines recommend eating at least two servings of fish a week. One note of caution, however: some fish (particularly swordfish, shark, king mackerel, and tilefish) have been found by the FDA to contain unusually high levels of mercury and other contaminants and therefore should not be consumed by children or by pregnant or nursing women.

Fresh Fish

When looking to purchase seafood, make sure it is fresh and has been handled properly. One way to do this is to shop only at fish markets that you trust. I believe it is worth paying a little more to ensure that the quality is good; not only will the dish you are preparing taste better, you can also avoid getting extremely sick, as improperly handled fish and shellfish may contain parasites as well as toxins that can cause severe illnesses.

Whole fish should have bright red gills and clear, bulging eyes, with no strong fishy odors. Fresh fish fillets and steaks will appear moist and glistening throughout, with no apparent bruises or dark spots. At home, fish should be kept in the refrigerator at no higher than 38°F until ready to cook; however, between 30°F and 34°F is optimal.

Shellfish should be purchased still alive when possible, particularly lobsters, clams, and crabs. Clams, mussels, and cockles will remain closed if still alive (sometimes they open slightly, but will close again if pressed together). Shellfish may be stored at somewhat higher temperatures than fish, but around 40°F is best. Use all seafood as quickly as possible after buying, since it is often impossible to know how long ago it might have been caught.

One way to purchase fresh seafood and still save money is to try less expensive fish such as catfish, bluefish, or monkfish, or use calamari instead of shrimp. Who knows, you may even end up finding something you really like!

Now You're Cooking

Pan roasting is a common and effective method for cooking fish in restaurants. First, preheat the oven to 400°F. Then heat an ovenproof pan (I prefer stainless steel) on medium-high on the stovetop, add approximately 1 tablespoon of oil, and sear the fish on one side until golden brown. Turn the fish over and immediately place into the oven, cooking until it is opaque throughout if preparing white fish such as bass or halibut (usually about 5 to 7 minutes) or until the desired temperature is reached for fish such as salmon and tuna.

I have recommended pan roasting for both Sea Scallops with Mushroom Tortellini (page 78) and Pan-Seared Monkfish with (Not Your Mother's) Peas and Carrots (page 95) in this chapter. In addition to helping fish turn out beautifully, it has the added benefit of freeing up stovetop space for cooking side dishes and heating up other ingredients. However, there are many other low-fat ways to prepare fish and seafood, including baking, grilling, sautéing, broiling, steaming, and poaching.

Whichever way you plan on preparing your fish or shellfish, there is no getting around the fact that it is a positive addition to any diabetic diet.

Steamed Mussels Hot Pot with Sake Broth

Prince Edward Island mussels, which are far less expensive than clams, oysters, or shrimp, are one of my favorite varieties. Imported New Zealand mussels are also excellent and have an attractive green shell, but they normally cost more than Prince Edward Island mussels and can be harder to find.

MAKES 4 APPETIZER SERVINGS

1 pound Prince Edward Island mussels, cleaned
2 tablespoons unsalted butter
2 tablespoons chopped lemongrass
2 tablespoons chopped ginger
2½ cups Sake Broth (page 47)
2 tablespoons chopped scallions, green parts only
Kosher salt
Freshly milled white pepper

1. To clean the mussels, soak them briefly in cold water to remove any grit; mussels with shells that remain open after cleaning are dead and should be discarded. Just before using the mussels, rip out the inedible "beard" (a tangle of threads that sticks out of the shell).
2. Melt 1 tablespoon of butter in a large sauté pan. Add the mussels and toss to coat. Add the lemongrass, ginger, and sake broth and simmer covered until the mussels open, approximately 4 minutes. Do not allow the broth to come to a full boil, as it will become cloudy and lose its visual appeal.
3. Add the scallions and the remaining butter, season with salt and pepper to taste, and serve hot.

Grilled Shrimp with Shaved Fennel

I created this dish while working as the chef of a popular restaurant in Brooklyn. It employs the basic philosophy of Italian cooking: use the freshest ingredients possible and let their natural flavors shine through clearly. Here, the licorice taste of the fennel, combined with mint and citrus, brightens and enhances the shrimp.

MAKES 5 APPETIZER SERVINGS

Grilled Shrimp
>   15 jumbo shrimp, peeled and deveined
>   3 tablespoons extra-virgin olive oil
>   2 rosemary sprigs
>   2 thyme sprigs
>   2 shallots, chopped

Shaved Fennel
>   6 tablespoons extra-virgin olive oil
>   1 tablespoon white wine vinegar
>   1 tablespoon fresh lemon juice
>   1 tablespoon fresh lime juice
>   1 tablespoon fresh orange juice plus 3 oranges, segmented
>   1 teaspoon kosher salt
>   ½ teaspoon freshly milled black pepper
>   2 fennel bulbs, shaved thin
>   ½ bunch mint leaves, chiffonade

1. Marinate the shrimp with olive oil, rosemary, thyme, and shallots in a bowl for approximately 1 hour in the refrigerator.
2. To make the shaved fennel, combine the extra-virgin olive oil and vinegar with the lemon, lime, and orange juices in a separate bowl and season with salt and pepper. Add the orange segments, fennel, and mint.
3. Brush the shrimp with olive oil, season lightly with salt and pepper, and grill over medium heat on a grill pan or outdoor barbecue until cooked through, approximately 2 minutes per side.

4. To serve, place the shaved fennel in the center of the plate, reserving the liquid. Place the shrimp on top and drizzle the liquid around the plate.

Variation: The shrimp can also be prepared in a sauté pan on medium heat until cooked through, approximately 2 minutes per side.

Grilled Shrimp with Lentil Ragout

Lentils are full of soluble fiber, complex carbohydrates, and protein and contain almost no fat, making them an ideal part of any healthful diabetic diet. They are also rich in iron and folic acid.

MAKES 5 APPETIZER SERVINGS

Grilled Shrimp
15 jumbo shrimp, peeled and deveined (see note)
3 tablespoons extra-virgin olive oil
2 rosemary sprigs
2 thyme sprigs
2 shallots

Lentil Ragout
2 tablespoons grapeseed oil
1 tablespoon chopped onion
2 teaspoons chopped celery
2 teaspoons chopped carrots
2 garlic cloves, minced
1 teaspoon kosher salt
½ teaspoon freshly milled black pepper
1 cup green or brown lentils
¼ cup white wine
2 cups chicken stock
1 tablespoon chopped cilantro
1 tablespoon chopped flat-leaf parsley
1 lemon

1. Marinate the shrimp with olive oil, rosemary, thyme, and shallots in the refrigerator for approximately 1 hour.
2. For the lentil ragout, warm a sauté pan on medium heat for 3 minutes. Add the grapeseed oil, followed by the onion, celery, carrots, garlic, salt, and pepper. Cook the vegetables until tender but not brown, approximately 4 minutes.
3. Add the lentils and cook until they become lightly toasted, 4 to 5 minutes. Deglaze with white wine. Add the chicken stock and simmer until the lentils are tender but not mushy, approximately 30 minutes more.

4. Add the cilantro and parsley and set aside in a warm area. (If desired, omit the cilantro and add an extra tablespoon of chopped parsley.) Taste the mixture and add additional seasoning if necessary.
5. Brush the shrimp with olive oil, season lightly with salt and pepper, and grill over medium heat on a grill pan or outdoor barbecue until cooked through, approximately 2 minutes per side.
6. Serve the shrimp on a bed of the lentil ragout, with a lemon wedge for garnish.

Note: Ask your fishmonger to peel and devein the shrimp for you, which can be done quickly and efficiently, and usually at no extra cost.

Grilled Calamari with Cucumber-Tomato Salad

Calamari (squid) is very inexpensive—especially when compared with the cost of shrimp or scallops—and, like any other seafood, it is high in protein and low in fat.

MAKES 4 APPETIZER SERVINGS

Calamari
    12 calamari, tubes and tentacles
    3 tablespoons extra-virgin olive oil
    2 rosemary sprigs
    2 thyme sprigs
    2 shallots, chopped

Vinaigrette
    6 tablespoons extra-virgin olive oil
    2 tablespoons red wine vinegar
    1 teaspoon kosher salt
    ½ teaspoon freshly milled white pepper

Cucumber-Tomato Salad
    2 medium tomatoes, seeded
    1 English cucumber, peeled and seeded
    3 tablespoons chopped basil

1. Marinate the calamari tubes and tentacles with olive oil, rosemary, thyme, and shallots in the refrigerator for 3 to 4 hours before cooking.
2. To make the vinaigrette, combine the extra-virgin olive oil and vinegar in a bowl and season with salt and pepper.
3. For the tomato-basil salad, cut the tomatoes and cucumber into medium dice. Toss the tomatoes, cucumber, and basil with the vinaigrette.
4. Brush the calamari with olive oil, season lightly with salt and pepper, and grill over medium heat on a grill pan or outdoor barbecue until opaque, 1 to 2 minutes per side (be careful not to overcook the calamari, or they will become tough and rubbery).

5. Spoon the cucumber-tomato salad onto a plate and place the grilled calamari around the salad. Pour some of the remaining vinaigrette over the calamari.

Variation: A combination of grilled scallops, shrimp, or a mixture of all three will work well for this dish. In addition, frozen calamari may be used in place of fresh in this recipe.

Lentil Linguini with White Clam Sauce

While this recipe calls for littleneck clams, Manila clams, and cockles, it is fine to use only littleneck clams if the others are unavailable. Cherrystone clams may also be substituted without any loss of flavor, but they will be chewier.

MAKES 4 SERVINGS

1 dozen littleneck clams
1 dozen Manila clams
1 dozen cockles
3 tablespoons extra-virgin olive oil
Kosher salt
8 ounces lentil linguini (see note)
1 small onion, small dice
3 garlic cloves, minced
½ cup white wine
One 8-ounce can clam juice
2 tablespoons unsalted butter, optional
½ bunch flat-leaf parsley, chopped
Freshly milled white pepper

1. Scrub the clamshells well with a brush and rinse under cold water to remove any grit.
2. Bring 1 gallon of water to a boil in a large pot. Add 1 tablespoon of olive oil and 1 tablespoon of salt to the water. Add the pasta and cook until just al dente, approximately 10 minutes, and then strain through a colander.
3. While the pasta is cooking, heat the remaining 2 tablespoons of olive oil in a large pan. Add all the littleneck clams, Manila clams, and cockles to the pan. Add the onion and garlic and toss everything together.
4. Slowly pour in the wine and bring to a boil. Add the clam juice and return the liquid to a boil; cover the pan until the clams and cockles open, approximately 2 to 4 minutes.
5. Remove and reserve the clams and cockles in their shells when they open and return any remaining liquid to the pan.

6. Add the pasta to the broth and cook 2 minutes longer. Add the clams, butter (if using), and parsley to the pan just before serving and season with salt and pepper to taste.

Note: Lentil linguini is a gluten-free pasta made from lentils. It can be found at most health food stores or on the Internet.

Variation: To make your own clam juice at home, purchase 6 to 8 chowder clams, scrub the shells thoroughly with a brush, and steam them in a pot with ¼ cup water until they open, approximately 10 minutes. Discard the shells and strain the liquid through a fine mesh strainer wrapped with cheesecloth to remove any remaining grit. The chowder clams may be chopped up and added to the dish if desired.

Grilled Scallops with Pea Foam

Many high-end chefs like to show off by using foams in their cooking, but the pea foam in this dish is amazingly simple to prepare, and the method can be replicated with a number of other vegetables, including asparagus and leeks.

MAKES 4 SERVINGS

12 large dry sea scallops (see note)
2 tablespoons grapeseed oil
Kosher salt
Freshly milled white pepper
One 10-ounce box frozen peas
½ cup skim milk
2 tablespoons unsalted butter
1 cup Three-Bean Salad with Ginger-Lemon Vinaigrette (page 33)

1. Preheat a grill pan or outdoor grill. Brush the scallops with the grapeseed oil and season liberally with salt and pepper.
2. Grill the scallops until medium (slightly translucent on the inside), approximately 3 minutes per side. To check for doneness, press down lightly on the scallops with your fingers—they should give slightly but spring back to their original shape.
3. For the pea foam, heat the peas and skim milk together in a small pot just to a simmer and immediately remove from the heat. Puree in a blender and strain. Add the butter, and salt and pepper to taste. Return the mixture to the blender and pulse to form a foam.
4. Spoon the pea foam over the scallops and serve alongside the Three-Bean Salad for a beautiful contrast of flavor, color, and texture.

Note: Be certain to ask for dry sea scallops only. Normally, scallops are soaked in a water and phosphate solution, which prolongs their shelf life and increases their size, but these wet scallops give off added moisture that prevents them from browning properly. I also think dry scallops taste much better, although they do cost more. Wet scallops can usually be identified by their unnaturally white color. Scallops should not smell fishy when purchased, and as they spoil quickly, it is best to use them within 1 to 2 days.

Sea Scallops with Mushroom Tortellini

Wonton wrappers are a great way for the home cook to prepare fresh pasta with a minimum amount of effort. They are available at any grocery store selling Asian products, some supermarkets, and online from a number of sources.

MAKES 5 SERVINGS

Kosher salt
4 bunches flat-leaf parsley
Freshly milled white pepper
1 package square egg wonton wrappers
2 cups Mushroom Puree (page 53)
2 tablespoons extra-virgin olive oil
15 large sea scallops (see note)

1. Bring a large pot of salted water to a boil, cover, and set aside until ready to use for the pasta.
2. For the parsley water, place the parsley into a blender and add 1 cup of cold water. Blend together with salt and pepper to taste, then strain the mixture through a colander wrapped in cheesecloth. Refrigerate the parsley water until ready to use.
3. For the pasta, place a wonton wrapper on a cutting board or other flat surface and spoon approximately 1 teaspoon of Mushroom Puree in the center.
4. Fold the wontons into a triangle shape and use a pastry brush or your finger to dab water onto the edges of the dough to seal. Then bring the two points at the base of the triangle together to create the tortellini.
5. For the scallops, preheat the oven to 400°F. Heat a stainless steel, ovenproof sauté pan on medium-high until very hot, approximately 5 minutes.
6. Pour the olive oil into the pan and immediately add the scallops. Sear them on one side until golden brown, about 3 minutes. Meanwhile, add the tortellini to the pot of boiling water.
7. Turn the scallops over and place them (still in the pan) into the oven for approximately 4 minutes. Do not overcook the scallops or

they will become rubbery—they should spring back slowly if pressed down on with your finger, and when cut open they will still appear slightly translucent in the center.

8. Cook the tortellini in the boiling water until they begin to float to the surface, approximately 3 minutes. Drain and toss them in a small amount of olive oil, and add salt and pepper to taste.

9. To serve, place some tortellini in the bottom of each bowl. Rest three scallops against the pasta and drizzle some of the parsley water over the dish.

Note: Be certain to ask for dry sea scallops only. Normally, scallops are soaked in a water and phosphate solution, which prolongs their shelf life and increases their size, but these wet scallops give off added moisture that prevents them from browning properly. I also think dry scallops taste much better, although they do cost more. Wet scallops can usually be identified by their unnaturally white color. Scallops should not smell fishy when purchased, and as they spoil quickly, it is best to use them within 1 to 2 days.

Variation: If you want to avoid the extra step of making the tortellini, simply leave the pasta in a triangle shape. The dish will taste just as good, and the cooking time for the pasta will be the same.

New England Lobster Maki

The traditional New England lobster roll gets a decidedly Asian twist in this recipe, which calls for a number of ingredients used in Japanese cooking: miso-based Kewpie Mayonnaise, white soy sauce, sweet cooking rice wine, and wasabi tobiko (spicy fish roe eggs). These products can be found in stores specializing in Asian products or from a number of online sources.

MAKES 10 SERVINGS

Ten 1-pound female lobsters (see note)
1 bunch celery, small dice (2 cups)
1 English cucumber, peeled and seeded, medium dice
2 cups Hellmann's Mayonnaise
4½ teaspoons Old Bay seasoning
Kosher salt
Freshly milled white pepper
2 Hass avocados, medium dice
1 cup Kewpie Mayonnaise
4 tablespoons white soy sauce
½ cup sweet cooking rice wine
¾ cup wasabi tobiko, optional
1 teaspoon unsalted butter
Ten 1-foot hot dog buns
Red pepper, julienned
Cilantro, picked
Lemon segments

1. Boil the lobsters in a large pot for 8 minutes (prepare in batches if necessary). The flesh should be white (opaque) throughout. Remove the meat from the claws and tails, cut into small bite-size pieces, and refrigerate to cool.
2. Mix together the celery, cucumber, Hellmann's Mayonnaise, Old Bay seasoning, and salt and pepper to taste. Fold in the avocado.
3. In a separate bowl, stir the Kewpie Mayonnaise together with the soy sauce, rice wine, and tobiko if using, and combine with the lobster and celery, cucumber, and avocado mixture.

4. Lightly butter the inside of the hot dog buns and grill or toast until brown. Fill a bun with lobster meat and garnish with red pepper julienne, cilantro, and lemon segments.

Note: I like to use female lobsters when available, because I find that their meat tends to be sweeter; however, either male or female lobsters are fine.

Fluke Tartare and Cucumber-Radish Salad

Even if the idea of eating raw fish does not sound tempting, this dish may still appeal to you. The fluke is "cooked" in lemon juice, and the acid in the juice turns the flesh white. The key to success is to find the freshest fish possible—be sure to visit a trusted store, and ask for sushi-grade fish.

MAKES 6 APPETIZER SERVINGS

1 pound fluke fillet, sushi grade
2 Meyer lemons (see note)
¼ cup extra-virgin olive oil
Kosher salt
Freshly milled white pepper
1 bunch radishes
1 English cucumber, peeled and seeded
¼ cup chopped basil

1. Dice the fluke and mix with the juice of 1 Meyer lemon and 2 tablespoons of extra-virgin olive oil. Season with salt and pepper to taste and refrigerate immediately.
2. Shave the radishes and cucumber using a mandoline. Segment the remaining lemon and place in a bowl with the radish and cucumber. Add basil and the remaining extra-virgin olive oil and mix together. Season with salt and pepper to taste.
3. Serve the cucumber-radish salad with the tartare for a cool, refreshing summertime dish.

Note: Meyer lemons can be hard to find, especially if they are not in season, but regular lemons may be used instead. If using regular lemon juice, which is less sweet, it is a good idea to cut back on the quantity a bit; let your taste buds be the judge.

Variation: Fluke is available in many fish stores, but sushi-grade salmon, tuna, or scallops work just as well in this dish.

Grilled Salmon with Slow-Cooked Fennel and Cucumber-Yogurt Sauce

This dish is quick and easy to prepare on a weeknight, but it is also elegant enough to serve at an elaborate dinner party. While the fennel is cooking you can prepare the rest of the dish, and everything will be ready in about an hour.

MAKES 4 SERVINGS

Slow-Cooked Fennel
½ cup extra-virgin olive oil
1 tablespoon fresh lemon juice
1 tablespoon white wine vinegar
1 fennel bulb, small dice
1 yellow onion, small dice
1 thyme sprig
Kosher salt
Freshly milled white pepper

Cucumber-Yogurt Sauce
Kosher salt
1 English cucumber, peeled and seeded
1 cup low-fat yogurt
2 garlic cloves, minced
½ bunch dill, chopped
1 tablespoon ground cumin
Freshly milled white pepper

Salmon
Four 6-ounce salmon fillets
3 tablespoons extra-virgin olive oil
Kosher salt
Freshly milled white pepper

1. For the slow-cooked fennel, combine the olive oil, lemon juice, vinegar, fennel, onion, and thyme in a nonreactive saucepan and cook on low heat until the fennel is soft, about 1 hour. Season with salt and pepper to taste.

2. To make the cucumber-yogurt sauce, grate the cucumber using a cheese grater. Mix the cucumber with 1 teaspoon of salt, let it drain for 20 minutes in a colander, and then squeeze the remaining liquid out. Mix the cucumber together with the yogurt and season with garlic, dill, cumin, salt, and pepper to taste.
3. Brush the salmon lightly with olive oil and season with salt and pepper. Grill over a medium flame, turning once halfway through, until desired temperature is reached.
4. Spoon 2 ounces of the yogurt sauce onto the center of a plate. Using a slotted spoon, place some of the fennel-onion mixture on top of the yogurt and rest a piece of the grilled salmon over that. Brush the salmon lightly with a little of the oil from the fennel-onion mixture and serve.

Steamed Bass with Shiitake Mushrooms and Baby Bok Choy

The method used in this recipe of steaming mild, flaky fish (such as black sea bass and cod) over broth is very popular in Asian cooking. It results in flavorful fillets that are moist and delicate, without the addition of any fat.

MAKES 6 SERVINGS

1 cup chopped ginger
1 cup chopped garlic cloves (from 6 heads garlic)
1 cup low-sodium soy sauce
Three 4-ounce black bass fillets, skin removed
Kosher salt
Freshly milled white pepper
2 bunches baby bok choy, sliced
20 shiitake mushrooms (stems removed), sliced
2 cups Sake Broth (page 47)

1. Place a steamer basket into a pot filled with the ginger, garlic, soy sauce, and 2 cups of water. Be careful not to let the liquid touch the bottom of the basket.
2. Season the fish fillets with salt and pepper to taste on both sides. Lay the bok choy onto the bottom of the basket and place the fish over the bok choy; top with the shiitakes and cover the pot with a tight-fitting lid.
3. Bring the cooking liquid to a simmer and steam until the flesh is white and flaky, approximately 4 to 5 minutes. In a separate pot, heat the sake broth just to a simmer.
4. To serve, place the mushrooms in the bottom of a bowl and top with the bok choy and fish. Pour some sake broth into the bowl and enjoy.

Note: The broth used for steaming is highly seasoned so that it will perfume the fish while it is cooking, but it is too strongly flavored to drink by itself.

Variation: If you cannot find shiitake mushrooms, replace with 2 portobello mushrooms (stems removed), sliced. Alternatively, approximately 3 ounces dried shiitake mushrooms may be substituted—just soak the dried mushrooms in ½ cup warm water for 30 minutes before preparing the dish.

Red Snapper in Tomato-Saffron Broth

Saffron may be the most expensive spice, but it usually only requires a few pinches to flavor a dish, and the results are always impressive. Saffron is the stigma (inside of the flower) of a certain type of crocus, and these stigmas must be picked by hand and then dried before packaging. No wonder it's so expensive!

MAKES 6 SERVINGS

10 plum tomatoes
1 cup Sacramento tomato juice or low-sodium tomato juice
1 garlic clove, smashed
1 tablespoon saffron
Kosher salt
Freshly milled white pepper
3 tablespoon extra-virgin olive oil
Six 6-ounce red snapper fillets, skin on
1 pint Artichoke Oreganata Puree (page 62)

1. For the tomato broth, cut the tomatoes into quarters lengthwise and scoop out the seeds with a knife; discard the seeds. Puree the tomatoes in a blender and then add the tomato juice and 1 cup of water.

2. Pour the puree into a pot and add garlic, saffron, and salt and pepper to taste. Bring the mixture to a boil and then transfer to a plastic or stainless steel container, or a glass or ceramic bowl.

3. Cool the liquid until it begins to separate. Slowly strain through a fine mesh strainer, reserving the liquid.

4. Heat a stainless steel sauté pan on medium-high until very hot, approximately 5 minutes. Pour the olive oil into the pan; immediately add the red snapper fillets, skin side down. Cook until the bottom of the fish begins to curl up around the edges, approximately 5 minutes. Turn the fish over and continue cooking until the flesh is opaque throughout, about 2 minutes more.

5. To serve, place a dollop of the Artichoke Oreganata Puree in the center of the bowl. Spoon some broth around the bowl and place the fish on top.

Variation: Red snapper is one of the more common fish available today in most parts of the United States, but other fish that will work just as well in this dish include black sea bass and striped bass.

Grilled Halibut and Buckwheat Salad

Roasted buckwheat (kasha) is commonly used in Eastern European cooking. It is treated as a grain and can be cooled after cooking and mixed with vegetables and other ingredients to form a nutritious salad like the one used in this dish.

MAKES 8 SERVINGS

½ cup kasha (makes 2 cups, cooked)
2 cups string beans, medium dice
4 medium tomatoes, medium dice
1 bunch flat-leaf parsley, chopped
2 bunches scallions, green parts only, chopped (1⅓ cups)
½ bunch mint, chiffonade
¼ cup fresh lemon juice (from 1 to 2 lemons)
½ cup extra-virgin olive oil
Kosher salt
Freshly milled white pepper
Eight 6-ounce halibut fillets

1. To prepare the buckwheat, bring 1 cup of water to a boil. Stir in the buckwheat, cover tightly, and simmer on very low heat until the grains become tender and all the liquid is absorbed, approximately 6 to 8 minutes.
2. Allow the buckwheat to cool and then toss together with the string beans, tomatoes, parsley, scallions, mint, lemon juice, and olive oil to make the salad. Season with salt and pepper to taste.
3. Brush the halibut lightly with olive oil and season with salt and pepper. Grill on a grill pan or outdoor barbecue, or sauté on both sides over medium heat, until cooked through, approximately 4 minutes per side.
4. To serve, place the fish on top of the salad. Garnish with parsley.

Variation: An equal amount of wheat berries may be used in place of buckwheat in this recipe. Both buckwheat and wheat berries are loaded with soluble fiber, which helps regulate blood sugar levels and makes them a great choice for diabetics.

Olive-Oil-Poached Halibut with Braised Fennel

The method of poaching fish in olive oil is far healthier than it might sound. Firm fish such as halibut will not soak up much oil during poaching, and as long as it is dabbed dry with a paper towel after cooking, there will be no more oil than if the fish were sautéed. Poaching in olive oil also ensures that the fish will remain moist and flavorful.

MAKES 4 SERVINGS

1 cup extra-virgin olive oil
1 tablespoon fresh lemon juice
1 tablespoon white wine vinegar
1 fennel bulb, small dice
1 yellow onion, small dice
¼ cup brine-cured black olives (see note)
1 thyme sprig
1 medium tomato, diced
Kosher salt
Freshly milled white pepper
Four 6-ounce halibut fillets
1 lemon

1. For the braised fennel, preheat the oven to 350°F. Combine the olive oil, lemon juice, vinegar, fennel, onion, olives, and thyme in a baking dish and cook in the oven until the fennel becomes soft, approximately 1 hour. (Including the olives with the fennel early on will intensify the flavor of the dish; however, they may be added at any time during the cooking process.) Add the tomatoes and season with salt and pepper to taste.

2. Strain the leftover olive oil from the fennel and reserve. Set aside the vegetables in a warm spot while preparing the fish.

3. Return the excess olive oil to the pot. Using a cooking thermometer to check the temperature of the oil (it should remain between 160°F and 180°F), poach the fish until cooked through, approximately 15 minutes. Remove the fish and pat off any excess oil with a paper towel.

4. To serve, spoon some of the braised fennel mixture onto a plate and place a halibut fillet on top. Garnish with a lemon wedge.

Note: Kalamata, Gaeta, and Niçoise are a few of the many types of brine-cured olives that will work well with this dish. It is fine to purchase pitted olives, but I would not recommend most canned or jarred olives, as I find that both the flavor and texture tend to be inferior.

Black Sea Bass with Mediterranean Cucumber-Tomato Salad

Salads with cucumber and tomatoes as the primary ingredients are very common in Mediterranean cooking. They are particularly enjoyable when ripe, flavorful tomatoes are used. The salad used in this dish is light, refreshing, and healthy, making it an ideal summertime entree.

MAKES 4 SERVINGS

1 English cucumber, medium dice
2 medium tomatoes, medium dice
½ red onion, medium dice
¼ cup brine-cured black olives, pitted and julienne
½ bunch mint, chiffonade
1 tablespoon red wine vinegar
4 tablespoons extra-virgin olive oil
Kosher salt
Freshly milled white pepper
Four 6-ounce black sea bass fillets
Mint, optional

1. For the salad, combine the cucumber, tomatoes, red onion, olives, mint, vinegar, and olive oil and mix together in a bowl. Season with salt and pepper to taste.
2. Brush the fish lightly with olive oil, sprinkle with salt and pepper, and grill on a grill pan or outdoor barbecue until just cooked through, approximately 3 to 4 minutes per side.
3. To serve, spoon the salad onto a plate and place the grilled fish on top. Garnish with a chiffonade of mint if desired.

Variation: Bronzino, red snapper, or halibut also go well with the cucumber-tomato salad in this recipe. The cooking method for each is the same.

Grilled Bronzino with Burst Tomatoes and Basil-Cumin Pesto

Pesto is an uncooked Italian sauce traditionally made with fresh basil, olive oil, Parmesan, and pine nuts, and often served with penne, linguine, and other dry pastas. It also goes particularly well with chicken and seafood, including shrimp and firm white fish such as bronzino (Mediterranean bass). There are numerous variations of pesto, including ones made with parsley or arugula, and walnuts in place of pine nuts.

MAKES 8 SERVINGS

Grilled Bronzino
Eight 6-ounce bronzino fillets
1 teaspoon extra-virgin olive oil
1 tablespoon chopped thyme
Kosher salt
Freshly milled white pepper

Burst Tomatoes
1 cup extra-virgin olive oil
1 pint baby red tomatoes, refrigerated
1 pint yellow, grape, or cherry tomatoes, refrigerated (see note)
1 garlic clove, smashed
1 shallot, sliced
1 thyme sprig

Basil-Cumin Pesto
Kosher salt
1 cup basil leaves
¼ cup flat-leaf parsley
½ cup extra-virgin olive oil
1 tablespoon ground cumin
¼ cup pine nuts
2 tablespoons Parmesan, grated
Freshly milled white pepper

2 cups Cauliflower-Almond Puree (page 61)

1. Brush the bronzino lightly with olive oil, sprinkle with chopped thyme, and season with salt and pepper to taste. Grill on a grill pan or outdoor barbecue until just cooked through, approximately 4 minutes per side.
2. For the tomatoes, heat the olive oil in a pot until just simmering. Add the refrigerated red and yellow tomatoes (make sure the tomatoes are cold, or they will turn mushy), garlic, shallots, and thyme sprig and remove from the heat. Allow it to sit away from the heat for 10 minutes.
3. For the pesto, fill a bowl with ice water and reserve. Bring 1 quart of salted water to a boil, add the basil and parsley, and blanch for 1 minute.
4. Remove the basil and parsley and immediately transfer it to the bowl of ice water to stop the cooking process. Squeeze the herbs dry inside a paper towel and place them in a blender. Add the olive oil, cumin, pine nuts, and Parmesan and pulse just to combine. Season with salt and pepper to taste.
5. Warm the puree in a microwave on medium for 2 minutes, or heat in a saucepot on low until warm, approximately 4 minutes.
6. To serve, place a dollop of Cauliflower-Almond Puree in the center of a plate and drizzle some pesto around. Spoon a few tomatoes on the plate and place a piece of grilled fish on top of the puree.

Note: A mix of yellow and red baby tomatoes gives the dish added color, but if the yellow tomatoes are unavailable, it is fine to use red ones only. Either way, there will be plenty of oil left over in the pot when the tomatoes are finished cooking, and this oil can be strained and reused in other dishes.

Pan-Seared Monkfish with (Not Your Mother's) Peas and Carrots

Monkfish, or angler fish, is often referred to as "poor man's lobster" due to its firm texture and vaguely lobsterlike taste. The only part of the monkfish that is edible is the tail, which is served skinless and can be prepared using a variety of cooking methods, including searing, baking, and steaming.

MAKES 8 SERVINGS

Eight 6-ounce monkfish fillets
Kosher salt
Freshly milled white pepper
2 tablespoons clarified butter (page 15)
½ cup sugar snap peas
½ cup snow peas
1 cup baby carrots
1 tablespoon chopped ginger
2 tablespoons unsalted butter
2 tablespoons water
1 tablespoon thyme
1 tablespoon truffle oil

1. Preheat the oven to 400°F. Heat an ovenproof stainless steel sauté pan on medium-high until hot, approximately 4 minutes. Season the fish with salt and pepper to taste.
2. Pour the clarified butter into the pan and sear the fish until golden brown on all sides. Place the pan in the oven and cook until the fish is firm and opaque throughout, approximately 10 minutes.
3. While the fish is cooking, blanch and shock the sugar snap peas, snow peas, and baby carrots. Heat a sauté pan on medium and add the ginger and unsalted butter first. As soon as the butter melts, add the vegetables and toss everything together. Pour in 2 tablespoons of water and sauté until the vegetables are warmed through, an additional 2 to 3 minutes. Season with salt and pepper to taste.

4. When the fish is done, add the thyme to the sauté pan and baste the fish with the drippings.
5. To serve, spoon some of the vegetable mixture onto a plate and place the monkfish fillet on top. Drizzle a small amount of truffle oil over the fish.

Chapter

Poultry and Meat

Both poultry and meat are excellent sources of protein and other essential nutrients, but they are high in fat and cholesterol compared with fish, shellfish, and tofu. (Beef and lamb are especially high in fat and cholesterol.) However, some fat is necessary in any diet, and if poultry and meat are eaten in moderate amounts and combined with low-calorie foods such as vegetables, the potential to consume too much fat and cholesterol is minimized. One recipe that follows this formula is the Poached Filet Mignon with Asian Vegetables and Egg Noodles (page 117).

The cooking method used to prepare a dish also helps determine how much fat and cholesterol will end up in your body at the end of the day. For example, if a chicken cutlet is breaded and deep-fried, it will contain more fat (and calories) than if it is grilled or sautéed. Poaching and roasting can both be done without the addition of any fat, making them particularly desirable for a diabetic diet.

Is It Ready Yet?

For most meat and even some poultry, there is a range of suggested doneness, rather than one set temperature (in other words, some people like their filet mignon cooked rare, and others prefer it medium or even well done). Chefs often like to stay on the lower end of this range to maintain the juiciness and flavor of the product.

The United States Department of Agriculture recommends cooking all poultry to a minimum temperature of 180°F, but many chefs consider chicken and turkey to be done at 165°F. However, unless you really trust the source of your poultry, I suggest erring more toward the USDA guidelines. For lamb, the USDA minimum is 160°F, but 140°F is often preferred by professional cooks.

The most important reason to follow the USDA cooking guidelines is to avoid becoming sick from potentially contaminated items. Harmful bacteria in poultry and meat may include salmonella, *E. coli,* and listeria. Fresh pork is normally cooked to a minimum of 160°F to avoid the possibility of becoming infected with trichinosis.

In addition to poultry and meat, potential carriers of disease include dairy products, fish, shellfish, and tofu; more recently, raw vegetables have been singled out as possible causes of illness. In all cases, it is essential to purchase food only from reliable sources and to ensure that everything is stored properly and used within the recommended period of time.

One foolproof way to gauge the doneness of poultry and meat— including chicken, turkey, pork, lamb, and beef—is to use a cooking thermometer. Meat thermometers are normally inserted at the beginning and left in until the cooking process is complete. Instant-read thermometers give the temperature of meat in a few seconds and should not be left in the oven.

Helpful Hints

When preparing whole poultry, including chicken and turkey, I always truss the meat to ensure even cooking. To truss a chicken, tuck the wings behind the back, and then use a long piece of butcher's twine to tie both the legs and wings tightly against the body of the chicken. I recommend using this method for both the Slow-Roasted Chicken with Herb Spaetzle and Roasted Mushrooms (page 107) and

Roasted Chicken with Lemon-Sultana Compote and Roasted Peppers (page 111).

When poultry and especially meat has finished cooking, it is important to let it rest for a few minutes to allow the juices to redistribute. The juices flow to the center while cooking, and if poultry or meat is carved immediately, these juices will run out; resting allows the juices to redistribute. Times vary depending on the size and cut—for example, the Pan-Roasted Filet Mignon with Sautéed Mustard Greens (page 115) should only need 5 to 10 minutes to rest, but a large roast such as a steamship round might require up to an hour. Also keep in mind that there will be some "carryover" cooking after meat is removed from the oven and allowed to rest (as much as 15° F for larger roasts).

Keep It Balanced

One thing that poultry and meat do not contain is carbohydrates, and despite the importance of controlling the levels of carbohydrates for people with diabetes, they are a necessary component of any diabetic food plan. Remember, a diet featuring the proper balance of carbohydrates, fat, and protein—in the form of poultry, meat, fish, shellfish, and soy-based products such as tofu—is the key to a successful diabetic diet.

Beef Carpaccio with Jicama, Cucumber, and Watermelon

Jicama is a tuber with white, crisp flesh that is sweet and juicy (think of it as a cross between a cucumber and a water chestnut). Jicama is normally served raw, and in this dish it provides a crunchy contrast to the tender beef.

MAKES 6 APPETIZER SERVINGS

½ pound beef short loin, sliced paper thin (see note)
6 pieces seedless watermelon, sliced ⅛ inch thin (1 cup)
1 English cucumber, peeled, seeded and sliced thinly
½ pound jicama, peeled and sliced thinly
¼ cup extra-virgin olive oil
Coarse sea salt
Freshly milled black pepper
Basil leaves, chiffonade

1. Make sure the beef, watermelon, cucumber, and jicama are cold before preparing the dish (the beef should remain refrigerated at all times to maintain freshness).
2. Layer the beef, watermelon, cucumber, and jicama on a plate; begin with the cucumber slices on the bottom, followed by the watermelon and the jicama. Lay the beef slices on top and sprinkle the olive oil over the meat and around the plate. Season with salt and pepper to taste, and garnish with the basil chiffonade.

Note: The idea of eating raw beef may be worrisome to some, but it is no different from raw fish (sushi, anyone?). Steak tartare, made from raw beef, has long been a popular dish in French bistros, and beef carpaccio is very common in some regions of Italy. When purchasing meat for carpaccio, be sure to visit only a trusted butcher, and let the butcher know you will be serving the beef raw.

Lentils and Spanish Chorizo

Mexican chorizo (made with fresh pork) and Spanish chorizo are similarly spiced. However, I prefer Spanish chorizo for this dish because it is made with smoked pork, which goes particularly well with the earthy flavor of the lentils.

MAKES 6 APPETIZER SERVINGS

3 tablespoons extra-virgin olive oil
4 shallots, small dice (½ cup)
1 garlic clove, minced
½ carrot, small dice (¼ cup)
1 celery stalk, diced (¼ cup)
Kosher salt
Freshly milled black pepper
½ pound Spanish chorizo, small dice
1 pound green or brown lentils
½ bunch flat-leaf parsley, chiffonade
¼ cup fresh lemon juice (from 1 to 2 lemons)

1. Heat a saucepot on medium and add the olive oil. Add the shallots, garlic, carrots, and celery and season with salt and pepper to taste. Cook until the shallots are translucent, approximately 5 to 7 minutes. Remove the vegetables from the pan and reserve.
2. In the same pot, add the diced chorizo and sauté to render some of the fat, approximately 3 minutes. Add the lentils and toss to coat. Cover with ¼ cup of water and simmer until the lentils are cooked but not mushy, approximately 30 minutes.
3. Return the vegetables to the pot, stir together with the chorizo and lentils, and remove from the heat. Add the parsley and lemon juice, adjust seasoning if necessary, and serve as an appetizer or hearty side dish.

Variation: To turn this appetizer into a meal, add 12 raw, deveined large shrimp when returning the vegetables to the pot (see step 3). Cover and remove from the heat, and let stand for 5 minutes to cook the shrimp before adding the parsley and lemon juice. Mixing meat and seafood together may seem unusual, but a number of popular American dishes do with great success, including New England clam chowder and New Orleans–style gumbo.

Moo Shu Duck Confit

Duck confit is made by cooking the meat in its own fat and then covering and storing it in this fat. This method helps to both preserve and flavor the duck. While it is possible to make your own, packaged duck confit can also be excellent.

MAKES 12 APPETIZER SERVINGS

One package duck leg confit (6 legs) (see note)
2 bunches scallions, green parts only, julienne (1 cup)
1 red bell pepper, julienne (1 cup)
1 tablespoon hoisin sauce
12 moo shu wrappers (see note)
¼ cup toasted cashews, chopped

1. Microwave the duck confit on high for 1 minute. Use a spoon to scoop off the fat covering the outside of the duck. Pull the meat from the bones and shred it into bite-size pieces.
2. Heat a sauté pan on medium and cook the duck until warmed through, approximately 3 minutes. Mix the duck together with the scallions, red pepper, and hoisin sauce in a bowl.
3. Microwave the moo shu wrappers on high for 10 seconds, or warm in a preheated oven or toaster oven at 350°F for 1 minute.
4. Roll the duck mixture inside the moo shu wrappers and sprinkle with the cashews to garnish.

Note: Duck confit is available online, and increasingly from gourmet food stores; one popular brand is D'Artagnan (www.dartagnan.com). Moo shu wrappers are sold at food stores specializing in Asian products.

Variation: For a one-pot meal, add some Roasted Mushrooms (page 133) and julienne Napa cabbage to create a Duck and Wild Mushroom Wrap.

Variation: To turn this dish into hors d'oeuvres, chop up the ingredients and roll them inside the moo shu wrappers. Then cut each duck wrap across into bite-size pieces and serve individually.

Chicken Souvlaki with Cucumber-Yogurt Sauce and Greek Salad

Greek souvlaki traditionally uses lamb, but by substituting chicken breast this dish is lower in fat (and especially saturated fat). It is considered to be fast food in Greece, and in larger cities there are stands and takeout shops selling souvlaki everywhere.

MAKES 4 SERVINGS

Cucumber-Yogurt Sauce
1 cup nonfat yogurt
1 English cucumber, peeled and seeded
1 tablespoon kosher salt
1 tablespoon extra-virgin olive oil
1 tablespoon fresh lemon juice
½ bunch dill, picked
Pinch of cumin
Freshly milled white pepper

Chicken Souvlaki
¾ pound chicken breast, 1 inch cubed
¼ cup extra-virgin olive oil
¼ cup fresh lemon juice (from 1 to 2 lemons)
1 teaspoon dried oregano
Kosher salt
Freshly milled black pepper

Greek Salad
2 beefsteak tomatoes, sliced
1 English cucumber, peeled, seeded and sliced
4 ounces feta cheese, cubed
½ cup Kalamata olives, pitted
½ bunch mint, chiffonade
½ bunch flat-leaf parsley, chiffonade
¼ cup fresh lemon juice (from 1 to 2 lemons)
¼ cup extra-virgin olive oil
Kosher salt
Freshly milled white pepper
4 pitas, toasted

1. For the cucumber-yogurt sauce, place the yogurt into a colander lined with cheesecloth and allow to drain for approximately 30 minutes.

2. Slice the cucumber thinly, mix with salt, and drain in a separate colander for 30 minutes.

3. Squeeze any remaining water from the cucumber and combine with the drained yogurt, olive oil, lemon juice, dill, cumin, and white pepper to taste. Set aside in the refrigerator.

4. Marinate the chicken in olive oil, lemon juice, and oregano in the refrigerator for 2 hours maximum.

5. Heat a sauté pan on medium for 4 minutes. Season the chicken cubes liberally with salt and pepper. Sauté the chicken until browned and cooked through, approximately 5 to 7 minutes.

6. Toss the tomatoes, cucumber, feta, olives, mint, and parsley together in a bowl with the lemon juice and olive oil, and season with salt and pepper to taste. (Feta cheese and olives can be quite salty, so it is a good idea to taste the salad first before adding any additional salt.)

7. To serve, place the salad on a plate, top with some of the chicken cubes, and spoon the cucumber-yogurt sauce on top. Serve with toasted pita, if desired. (You can also use the pita to turn this dish into a filling sandwich.)

Chicken Paillard with Avocado-Tomatillo Salsa and Quinoa Pilaf

Quinoa was a staple of the ancient Incan diet. Today it is considered one of nature's healthiest foods, particularly for diabetics. In addition to being high in protein, quinoa is rich in fiber, vitamins, and minerals. It can be found in most health food stores and is available for purchase online.

MAKES 4 SERVINGS

Chicken Paillard
4 skinless chicken breasts (1½ pounds)
1 tablespoon extra-virgin olive oil
1 tablespoon chopped thyme

Avocado-Tomatillo Salsa
2 tablespoons Key Lime Avocado Oil, optional (see note)
1 avocado, diced
3 Key limes, segmented
5 tomatillos, chopped
1 red onion, diced
½ bunch cilantro, chopped
1 teaspoon kosher salt
½ teaspoon freshly milled black pepper

Quinoa Pilaf
1 garlic clove, minced
1 tablespoon small red onion, diced
1 cup quinoa
½ red pepper, small dice (¼ cup)
½ yellow pepper, small dice (¼ cup)

1. For the chicken, slice each breast in half lengthwise and place between two pieces of plastic wrap. Lightly pound the chicken with a mallet until approximately ¼ inch thin. Discard the plastic wrap and marinate the chicken with the olive oil and thyme in the refrigerator for 1 to 2 hours.

2. For the salsa, combine all the ingredients and macerate in the refrigerator for 2 to 3 hours before serving. This allows the flavors to distribute evenly.

3. For the quinoa, sweat the garlic and onion in 2 tablespoons of water in a small pot. Add the quinoa and 2 cups of water, along with a pinch of salt and pepper. Bring the water to a boil, reduce to a simmer, and cover for 15 minutes or until all the water has been absorbed. Turn off the flame, fluff the quinoa with a fork, and add the red and yellow peppers. Adjust the seasoning if necessary and set aside in a warm place.

4. Heat a pan on medium for 4 minutes. Sauté the chicken breasts until cooked through, approximately 3 to 4 minutes on each side.

5. Spoon some quinoa on the plate, top with the chicken, and spoon the salsa over the top and around the plate. Garnish with cilantro.

Note: Key Lime Avocado Oil may be purchased online from Pacifica Culinaria (www.pacificaculinaria.com).

Slow-Roasted Chicken with Herb Spaetzle and Roasted Mushrooms

Before roasting, the chicken is stuffed with lemon, thyme, and garlic. The flavor of these aromatics completely perfumes the chicken and gives it a fresh, lively flavor.

MAKES 4 SERVINGS

One 4-pound chicken
1 lemon
Kosher salt
Freshly milled white pepper
1 thyme sprig
2 garlic cloves, smashed
1 tablespoon extra-virgin olive oil
1 cup Herb Spaetzle (page 148)
1 cup Roasted Mushrooms (page 133)
Flat-leaf parsley

1. For the chicken, prick the lemon several times with a fork. Season the cavity with salt and pepper and stuff with the lemon, thyme, and garlic. Truss the chicken, brush the outside with olive oil, and season liberally with salt and pepper.
2. Preheat the oven to 350°F. Place the chicken on top of a roasting rack over a baking sheet and cook until the skin is golden brown, approximately 20 minutes. Turn the oven down to 300°F and continue cooking until the juices run clear, approximately 30 minutes longer. An instant-read thermometer can also be inserted into the chicken to check for doneness.
3. While the bird is cooking, prepare the Herb Spaetzle and Roasted Mushrooms according to the recipes provided and keep warm until ready to serve.
4. Remove the chicken from the oven when finished, allow it to cool slightly, and then separate the meat from the carcass with a knife.
5. Serve the chicken together with the Herb Spaetzle and Roasted Mushrooms and garnish with parsley.

Variation: To make a flavorful pan sauce, heat 1 cup of chicken stock and add the lemon and juices left over from the roasted chicken. Reduce the liquid slightly until thickened, and season with salt and pepper to taste. Strain through a fine mesh strainer, add some parsley leaves, and pour over the chicken.

Roasted Chicken with Herbes de Provence

Herbes de Provence—a mixture of dried spices including basil, marjoram, rosemary, sage, and lavender—is available at most supermarkets. In addition, espelette pepper is used to flavor the chicken in this dish; if unavailable, an equal amount of hot paprika can be substituted.

MAKES 4 SERVINGS

1 lemon
One 4-pound chicken
1 tablespoon herbes de Provence
1 teaspoon espelette pepper
2 thyme sprigs
2 garlic cloves, smashed
¼ cup extra-virgin olive oil
Sea salt
Freshly milled white pepper
8 fingerling potatoes, or 2 Yukon Gold potatoes (see note)
Flat-leaf parsley

1. Preheat the oven to 350°F. Prick the lemon several times with a fork. Next, season the cavity of the chicken with the herbes de Provence and ½ teaspoon of the espelette, and stuff with the lemon, thyme, and garlic.

2. Truss the bird (page 98), brush the outside with 2 tablespoons of olive oil, and season liberally with salt and pepper.

3. Place the chicken on top of a roasting rack over a baking sheet and roast until the skin is golden brown, approximately 20 minutes.

4. Turn the oven down to 300°F and continue cooking until the juices run clear, about 30 minutes longer. (An instant-read thermometer can also be inserted into the chicken to check for doneness.) When finished, allow the chicken to rest while preparing the rest of the dish.

5. For the fingerling potatoes, raise the oven temperature to 400°F and roast on a baking sheet until fork tender, approximately 10 to 12 minutes. If using Yukon Gold potatoes, first slice them into quarters lengthwise before roasting.

6. Using the back of a spoon, smash the roasted potatoes together with the remaining olive oil and espelette, and season with salt and pepper to taste.
7. Separate the meat from the carcass with a knife, slice, and serve alongside the smashed potatoes. Garnish with parsley.

Note: Fingerling potatoes (so named because they resemble gnarled fingers) and Yukon Gold potatoes are interchangeable in this recipe. Yukon Gold potatoes have become very popular in recent years and are often easier to find. Both varieties are ideal for roasting, or boiling and mashing, and are full of flavor.

Roasted Chicken with Lemon-Sultana Compote and Roasted Peppers

Sultanas are sweet yellow raisins that are difficult to find outside of a few gourmet retailers and online sources. However, golden raisins are readily available in supermarkets and make an acceptable substitute.

MAKES 4 SERVINGS

Roasted Chicken
1 lemon
One 4-pound chicken
Kosher salt
Freshly milled white pepper
1 thyme sprig
2 garlic cloves, smashed
1 tablespoon extra-virgin olive oil

Roasted Peppers
2 red bell peppers
1 garlic clove, minced
1 shallot, minced
1 tablespoon flat-leaf parsley, chiffonade

Lemon-Sultana Compote
2 tablespoons lemon zest
2 tablespoons sultana raisins, or 2 tablespoons golden raisins
2 tablespoons extra-virgin olive oil
2 tablespoons parsley
2 tablespoons red wine vinegar

1. For the chicken, prick the lemon several times with a fork. Season the cavity of the chicken with salt and pepper and stuff with the lemon, thyme, and garlic. Truss the chicken, brush the outside with approximately 1 tablespoon of olive oil, and season liberally with salt and pepper. Place on top of a roasting rack over a baking sheet and set aside.
2. Preheat the oven to 450°F. Place the red peppers on a baking sheet

in the oven and roast, turning occasionally, until the outsides are charred, approximately 10 to 15 minutes.

3. Lower the heat to 350°F and roast the chicken until the skin is golden brown, approximately 20 minutes. Turn the oven down to 300°F and continue cooking until the juices run clear, approximately 30 minutes longer. (An instant-read thermometer can also be inserted into the chicken to check for doneness.)

4. While the chicken is roasting, finish preparing the red peppers by peeling off the charred skin and discarding. Cut open the red peppers lengthwise and remove the seeds, ends, and white insides. Wipe the flesh clean with a paper towel and cut into julienne. Combine the roasted peppers with the garlic, shallots, and parsley, and set aside.

5. To prepare the Lemon-Sultana Compote, combine the lemon zest, sultanas, and olive oil in a saucepan. Heat everything on low until the sultanas plump up, about 2 minutes. Add the parsley, 1 tablespoon of vinegar, and salt and pepper to taste. Add more vinegar if necessary, then set aside.

6. Remove the chicken from the oven when finished, allow it to cool slightly, and separate the meat from the carcass with a knife.

7. Serve the chicken on a plate alongside the roasted peppers, with the compote spooned on top of the chicken.

Variation: The roasted chicken will also go great with the String Beans with Garlic and Almonds (page 134) in place of the Lemon-Sultana Compote.

Fragrant Spice-Rubbed Roast Pork Loin

While pork was once considered to be unhealthy in part because of its high fat content, the vast majority sold in the United States today is extremely lean. Pork loin is particularly low in fat, and as a result it normally requires a flavor boost such as the spice rub and oil used in this recipe (the oil also helps keep the meat moist).

MAKES 4 SERVINGS

One 1¼-pound boneless pork loin
6 cloves
2 garlic cloves, quartered
1 tablespoon plus 1 teaspoon ground cinnamon
2 teaspoons ground cumin
2 teaspoons ground coriander
1½ tablespoons extra-virgin olive oil
Kosher salt
Freshly milled black pepper

1. Roll up the pork loin and tie it together with butcher's twine (most butchers will do this for you, but you may have to call in advance and specify the size you want).
2. Preheat the oven to 350°F for 10 minutes. Meanwhile, push the cloves into the meat, spacing them at least 1 inch apart.
3. Next, cut 8 thin slits into the meat, using a paring knife, and place a piece of garlic into each one.
4. Stir the cinnamon, cumin, and coriander together with the olive oil, season with salt and pepper to taste, and use your fingers to rub this mixture onto the entire surface of the loin.
5. Place the pork loin on top of a roasting rack over a baking sheet in the oven and cook until it reaches an internal temperature of 145°F (use an instant-read thermometer to check for doneness).

6. Allow the meat to rest for 15 minutes to redistribute the juices. Remove the butcher's twine with scissors and cut the pork loin into approximately ¼-inch slices.

Variation: Another simple and healthful way to flavor pork loin is to marinate it in a 1-to-1 ratio of red wine vinegar and olive oil, along with rosemary, thyme, and garlic. Marinate the meat for 30 minutes in the refrigerator, and then roast it in a 450°F oven for 10 minutes.

Pan-Roasted Filet Mignon with Sautéed Mustard Greens

In addition to sautéed mustard greens, the filet mignon in this dish is paired with Roasted Mushrooms (page 133) and Truffle–Celery Root Puree (page 57). These full-flavored side dishes stand up well to the filet mignon and help cut its richness.

MAKES 4 SERVINGS

1 cup Roasted Mushrooms (page 133)
1 cup Truffle–Celery Root Puree (page 57)
Four 5-ounce portions filet mignon
Kosher salt
Freshly milled black pepper
2 tablespoons clarified butter (page 15)
1 thyme sprig
2 bunches mustard greens, chopped
2 tablespoons extra-virgin olive oil
1 garlic clove, chopped

1. Heat the Roasted Mushrooms and Truffle–Celery Root Puree in separate pots and keep warm until ready to serve.
2. Season the filet mignon liberally with salt and pepper. Heat a heavy-bottomed sauté pan on medium for approximately 5 minutes, add the clarified butter, and sear the meat on all sides. Add the thyme to the pan before finishing the last side.
3. After searing, baste the meat with the butter and juices (the longer the meat is basted, the more well done it will become). Set aside to rest for approximately 5 to 10 minutes before serving.
4. In a separate pan, sauté the mustard greens in the extra-virgin olive oil on medium until wilted, about 3 minutes, and add the garlic. Reduce heat to low, add approximately 1 tablespoon of water to the pan, and cover until cooked, 3 minutes more. Remove from the heat and set aside still covered.

5. To serve, drain the mustard greens on a paper towel to remove any excess water. Combine the mustard greens with the Roasted Mushrooms and serve alongside the Truffle–Celery Root Puree and filet mignon.

Variation: Mustard greens, collard greens, dandelion, and kale are all bitter greens and are interchangeable in this recipe.

Poached Filet Mignon with Asian Vegetables and Egg Noodles

Any of the vegetables in this recipe can be replaced with more readily available choices such as spinach or broccoli. The tofu can be omitted altogether; however, it is high in protein and low in fat.

MAKES 4 SERVINGS

Egg Noodles
2 large eggs
1 tablespoon flour
1 tablespoon cornstarch
1 teaspoon sesame oil
Kosher salt, to taste
Freshly milled black pepper, to taste
1 tablespoon canola oil

Filet Mignon
4 cups Basic Beef Stock (page 44)
1 tablespoon chopped ginger
2 bunches scallions, green parts only, julienne
2 garlic cloves
Four 3-ounce portions filet mignon

Asian Vegetables
½ cup snow pea pods, blanched
½ cup baby bok choy, sliced
½ cup mung bean sprouts
One 8-ounce package firm tofu, diced

1. For the noodles, combine the eggs, flour, cornstarch, sesame oil, salt, and pepper in a blender and run on high until the mixture becomes homogeneous and thickens slightly, about 5 minutes. Let it sit for 1 hour in the refrigerator to settle.
2. Heat a sauté pan on medium until hot, approximately 4 minutes. Pour in just enough canola oil to coat the bottom of the pan. Add a small amount of egg mixture, just enough to cover the bottom, and cook for 30 seconds on each side. Repeat until all the egg mix-

ture has been used, stacking the pancakes as you go. When finished, julienne the pancakes lengthwise, to resemble linguini strands, and set aside.

3. For the filet mignon, heat the beef stock to approximately 170°F (use an instant-read thermometer to gauge the temperature). Add the ginger, scallions, and garlic.

4. Place the filet mignon into the stock and poach until rare, approximately 7 minutes. Remove the meat and set aside.

5. For the Asian Vegetables, bring the broth to a boil and add the snow pea pods, baby bok choy, mung bean sprouts, tofu, and filet mignon. Cook for 3 minutes. Serve in a large bowl strewn with the egg noodles.

Prime Sirloin Steak with Vidalia Onion Jus

Vidalia onions are only available for a couple of months in the spring, and they are usually hard to find even then. But you can substitute any sweet onion for this recipe, such as Bermuda or Walla Walla.

MAKES 4 SERVINGS

2 Vidalia onions, medium dice
1 tablespoon extra-virgin olive oil
2 cups Basic Beef Stock (page 44)
Four 6-ounce prime sirloin steaks (see note)
Kosher salt
Freshly milled black pepper
2 cups Roasted Mushrooms (page 133)

1. For the jus, place the onions into a hot pan with the olive oil and sweat until translucent, approximately 5 minutes.
2. Reduce heat to low, stirring often, until the onions caramelize (approximately 25 minutes).
3. Deglaze the pan with the beef stock and reduce the liquid by one-third. Skim off any fat that accumulates on the surface with a ladle or spoon. Set the pan aside covered and in a warm spot.
4. Season the steak liberally with salt and pepper and cook on a grill pan or outdoor grill until it reaches the desired doneness— approximately 4 to 5 minutes per side for medium rare and 7 to 8 minutes per side for medium. Allow the meat to rest for 5 to 10 minutes before serving.
5. In a small pot, warm up the Roasted Mushrooms until hot and place them on the center of the plate. Top with the steak and spoon the onion jus on top.

Note: Steak is simple to prepare, so why can it taste so much better at a good restaurant or steakhouse than when you cook it at home? The main reason is quality!

To make sure your steak is top grade, ask the butcher for USDA prime meat only. The majority of steaks sold at supermarkets are the lower-quality choice grade, but you can usually find prime as well. You will pay more for prime meat, but since the portions are not very big in this recipe it shouldn't break the bank.

Flank Steak with Chinese Vegetables

All the ingredients used in this recipe are common in Chinese cooking, as is the method of stir-frying everything together in a wok. (Stir-frying is essentially the same as sautéing.)

MAKES 4 SERVINGS

1 pound flank steak, sliced thin (see note)
1 tablespoon low-sodium soy sauce
1 tablespoon cornstarch
1 tablespoon canola oil
1 tablespoon minced ginger
2 garlic cloves, minced
2 bunches scallions, green parts only, julienne
2 cups snow pea pods
1 cup baby bok choy, sliced
1 cup mung bean sprouts
One 8-ounce can water chestnuts
1 teaspoon sesame seeds
1 teaspoon sesame oil
Kosher salt
Freshly milled black pepper

1. Marinate the beef with the soy sauce and cornstarch for 20 minutes in the refrigerator. All of the soy sauce should be absorbed into the meat.
2. Heat a wok or large sauté pan on medium-high for 5 minutes. Add the canola oil and the ginger, garlic, and scallions, followed by the meat, and mix everything together.
3. Start adding the vegetables at 30-second intervals, beginning with the snow pea pods and followed by the bok choy, mung bean sprouts, and water chestnuts. Stir-fry until the beef is cooked through, 4 to 5 minutes total.
4. When finished, add the sesame seeds and sesame oil and season with salt and pepper to taste. Serve immediately to maintain the crispness of the vegetables.

Note: Flank steak is a leaner, tougher piece of meat than such popular cuts as filet mignon or rib eye. But flank steak is also full of flavor and far less expensive, and by slicing the meat thin and marinating it before cooking, it will become more tender. If desired, you can replace the flank steak with other cuts of beef such as filet mignon, rib eye, skirt steak, or hanger steak.

Seared Lamb Loin with Apple-Avocado Napoleon

We "eat with our eyes," so the appearance of a dish can be almost as important as how it tastes. In this case, the bright colors of the Apple-Avocado Napoleon and the accompanying Carrot-Ginger Puree offset the red lamb beautifully. Hungry yet?

MAKES 4 SERVINGS

2 cups Carrot-Ginger Puree (page 59)
1½ pounds lamb loin
Kosher salt
Freshly milled black pepper
2 tablespoons extra-virgin olive oil
2 rosemary sprigs
1 thyme sprig
1 celery root bulb, peeled
1 Granny Smith or other green apple
1 Hass avocado
Coarse sea salt

1. Preheat the oven to 400°F. In a small pot, heat the Carrot-Ginger Puree until warm; cover and set aside.
2. Season the lamb liberally on both sides with salt and pepper. Heat an ovenproof sauté pan on medium for 4 minutes, add the olive oil, and sear the meat on all sides.
3. Add 1 rosemary sprig and the thyme to the pan, baste the meat with the olive oil, and finish the lamb in the oven—7 minutes for medium rare, 9 minutes for medium. When finished, allow the meat to rest for 5 to 10 minutes in a warm spot.
4. While the lamb is still cooking, cut the celery root, apple, and avocado flesh into thin slices (do not cut the apple or avocado too far ahead, or they will turn brown when exposed to the air).
5. On a cutting board or other flat surface, layer the slices of celery root, apple, and avocado—start with some of the celery root on the bottom, followed by the apple, then the avocado, and finally the remaining celery root. Sear the napoleons on both sides in a sauté pan on the stovetop. (Alternatively, sear the celery root, apple, and

avocado slices briefly on one side, and cool before making the napoleons; preheat the oven to 350°F and bake the napoleon for 2 minutes to warm through.)

6. Place a napoleon on the side of each plate and spoon some of the Carrot-Ginger Puree next to it. Slice the lamb and lay it onto the plate. Sprinkle the coarse sea salt over the meat and napoleon, and garnish with the remaining rosemary sprig.

Lamb, Beet, and Goat Cheese Torta

Beets and goat cheese are a natural pairing: the sweetness of the roasted beets complements the tangy saltiness of the goat cheese perfectly. The lamb also goes well with the beets and goat cheese and helps make this dish a satisfying entrée.

MAKES 6 SERVINGS

2 medium beets
1 bunch asparagus
1 pound lamb loin
Kosher salt
Freshly milled black pepper
One 8-ounce log Coach Farms or other soft goat cheese
1 tablespoon chopped chives
1 tablespoon chopped thyme
1 tablespoon chopped flat-leaf parsley
6 flour tortillas
2 tablespoons extra-virgin olive oil
1 tablespoon 25-year-old balsamic vinegar, optional

1. Preheat the oven to 400°F. Wrap the beets individually in aluminum foil and roast in the oven until soft enough for a paring knife to pierce cleanly through the middle, approximately 40 to 45 minutes.
2. Meanwhile, blanch the asparagus in a large pot of boiling salted water, shock in ice water, and set aside on a paper towel.
3. Unwrap the beets and allow them to cool. Peel off the skin with a paring knife and cut the beets into thin slices.
4. Season the lamb liberally on both sides with salt and pepper. Cook on a grill pan or outdoor grill until rare, 5 minutes per side. Allow the meat to rest for 5 to 10 minutes, slice thinly, and reserve.
5. Mix the cheese and herbs together with a spoon. Place a tortilla onto a cutting board or other flat surface and spread the top lightly with a little of the goat cheese mixture. Place a few slices of lamb and beets over the goat cheese.
6. Place another tortilla on top, and repeat the process with each layer, covering everything with the final tortilla. Brush the top tortilla with

approximately 1 teaspoon of olive oil (not goat cheese) and cook
the torta in the oven until golden brown, approximately 5 minutes.

7. On a grill pan, grill the asparagus briefly on each side. Toss with
the remaining olive oil, balsamic vinegar if using, and salt and pepper to taste.

8. Carefully cut the torta into six pieces using a chef's knife and serve
hot alongside the asparagus.

Seared Duck Breast with Pumpkin-Seed Vinaigrette

Pumpkin-seed oil possesses a gorgeous dark green color and a rich, nutty flavor. It is also rich in omega-3 and other essential fatty acids. It is used regularly to flavor salads and garnish dishes in both German and Austrian cooking. Pumpkin-seed oil is available at some gourmet stores and online.

MAKES 4 SERVINGS

Pumpkin-Seed Vinaigrette
2 plum tomatoes
3 tablespoons honey
1 piece star anise
2 tablespoons sherry vinegar
2 tablespoons red wine vinegar
2 tablespoons balsamic vinegar
¼ cup pumpkin-seed oil
½ cup grapeseed oil
Kosher salt
Freshly milled black pepper
½ cup pumpkin seeds, toasted
1 cup Carrot-Ginger Puree (page 59)
1 cup Celery Root Puree (page 54)

Seared Duck Breast
1 pound duck breast
1 thyme sprig
1 rosemary sprig

1. For the vinaigrette, preheat the oven or toaster oven to 400°F. Slice the tomatoes and roast in the oven until browned and soft, approximately 10 to 15 minutes.
2. While the tomatoes are roasting, heat the honey in a small pot with the star anise until hot. Remove the star anise with a spoon and discard.
3. Place the tomatoes, anise honey, vinegars, pumpkin-seed oil, and grapeseed oil in a blender and process just to emulsify, approximately 1 minute. Season with salt and pepper to taste.

4. Crush the pumpkin seeds with a meat mallet or the side of a chef's knife and stir into the vinaigrette.

5. Heat the Carrot-Ginger Puree and Celery Root Puree in separate pots. Set aside, covered, in a warm spot.

6. For the duck, score the skin several times with a knife. In a cold pan on low heat, place the duck breast skin side down, and cook to render the fat from the skin.

7. When you start to see the fat accumulating (after about 5 minutes), add the thyme and rosemary to the pan and baste the flesh side repeatedly to flavor and cook the duck. (Warning: It is important to be extremely careful when cooking duck on the stovetop, as the fat can splatter and burn your skin if the pan becomes too hot.) Continue doing this until the meat is medium rare and the skin golden brown and crisp—approximately 6 minutes for rare or 9 minutes for medium. Discard the fat.

8. Allow the meat to rest for 5 minutes, then cut the breast across into several slices. Serve alongside the Carrot-Ginger Puree and Celery Root Puree. Finally, drizzle the vinaigrette over the duck and around the outside of the plate.

Chapter  7

Vegetables and Grains

The nutrients found in vegetables and grains, combined with protein-rich foods such as fish, poultry, and meat, make up the backbone of any healthful diabetic diet. Vegetables provide fiber as well as vitamins and minerals your body needs to stay healthy, and grains contain necessary fiber and other nutrients. Whether or not you have diabetes, vegetables and grains should constitute a substantial portion of your diet. And despite recent fad diets (particularly the Atkins Diet) that shun carbohydrates in favor of protein and fat, the fact remains that if you burn more calories than you eat per day, you will lose weight, no matter what foods you are consuming.

Eat Your Vegetables

Both meat and vegetables take up space in your stomach and make you feel full. Vegetables are much lower in calories, however, making them a healthy alternative for diabetics. By cutting down on the amount of meat and other fatty foods in your diet and adding more vegetables, it will be possible to lose weight, which should help control your blood sugar levels.

While vegetables do contain necessary vitamins and minerals, it is important to utilize the right cooking methods to retain these nutrients. One of my favorite ways to prepare vegetables is to stir-fry them in a wok or sauté pan; this allows the vegetables to cook quickly using a small amount of oil, and at the same time melds the flavors of all the different ingredients. Tofu and Vegetable Stir-Fry (page 147) is an especially healthy and flavorful example of this preparation. Steaming vegetables until just tender is another great way to keep in nutrients and flavor.

It is also important to eat different kinds of vegetables, which helps ensure that you are getting all the vitamins and minerals your body needs on a daily basis. For example, carrots are rich in vitamin A, and tomatoes are high in vitamin C. Some vegetables, including broccoli and spinach, are packed with a number of different vitamins and minerals. In my cooking, I like to combine several vegetables in one dish, which helps cover all the bases nutritionally and also provides variety to your diet; for example, Fettuccini with Asparagus, Morels, and Peas (page 152) contains plenty of nutrients and flavors, and I think it also tastes great.

Complex Grains

When eaten in moderation, bread, pasta, and rice are not unhealthy for diabetics to consume, especially if they are high in fiber. High-fiber grains include whole wheat, oats, brown rice, and barley. Lentils are also a great source of fiber and one of my favorite foods; they are used throughout this book, including in the Lentils and Spanish Chorizo recipe (page 101). However, refined starches, which include white bread and white rice, should for the most part be avoided, as they have been stripped of fiber and many of their nutrients.

There are two kinds of fiber in foods, insoluble fiber and soluble fiber, both of which help the body's digestive system function properly. Soluble fiber is especially important for diabetics, because it has been found to help control blood sugar levels and keep your blood cholesterol levels in check. Soluble fiber is present in such foods as beans, oats, and barley; many fruits and vegetables also contain both types of fiber.

Research has found that most people would benefit from consuming 25 to 35 grams of fiber a day. Unfortunately, most of us do not even consume half this much. To even come close to reaching this level on a daily basis, it is very important to keep an eye on what you eat. This means there is no room for empty calories from sugar and other simple carbohydrates, unless you want to end up gaining weight instead of losing it.

A Well-Balanced Diet

By consuming a nutritionally balanced meal that includes a variety of vegetables, whole grains packed with fiber, and foods high in protein, as well as limiting your overall calorie intake, it is possible for both diabetics and nondiabetics to begin losing weight, feel healthier, and ultimately live longer.

Marinated Mushroom Antipasto

These mushrooms are a good accompaniment to almost any entree. Alternatively, they can be served as an appetizer in the summer, either by themselves or with other cold vegetables including the Three-Bean Salad with Ginger-Lemon Vinaigrette (page 33). One advantage to this dish is that it can be made up to 3 days ahead and refrigerated until ready to use.

MAKES 10 SERVINGS

¼ cup extra-virgin olive oil
2 tablespoons red wine vinegar
1 teaspoon red pepper flakes
2 cups white button mushrooms, cleaned and quartered
1 cup crimini mushrooms, cleaned and quartered (see note)
Kosher salt
Freshly milled black pepper
2 tablespoons chiffonade flat-leaf parsley

1. Whisk together the olive oil, vinegar, and red pepper to make a vinaigrette. Toss the mushrooms with half of the vinaigrette and set aside for 2 hours in the refrigerator to marinate.
2. Preheat the oven to 450°F. Transfer the mushrooms to a sheet pan and roast in the oven until browned, approximately 10 minutes. Remove the mushrooms from the oven and allow them to cool to room temperature.
3. Toss the roasted mushrooms together with the remaining vinaigrette, season with salt and pepper to taste, and stir in the parsley just before serving.

Note: Crimini mushrooms are darker and have an earthier flavor than button mushrooms, but in appearance they are almost the same. If you are unable to find criminis, it is fine to use a total of 3 cups of button mushrooms for this recipe.

Roasted Mushrooms

Mushrooms benefit particularly well from roasting, which helps intensify their flavor and produces an attractive brown exterior. Roasted mushrooms go particularly well with beef dishes such as Pan-Roasted Filet Mignon (page 115).

MAKES 4 SERVINGS

1 tablespoon grapeseed oil
1 tablespoon chopped white onion
2 garlic cloves, chopped
15 to 20 white button mushrooms, chopped (2 cups)
¼ cup white wine
½ cup chicken stock
1 tablespoon unsalted butter
1 tablespoon chopped flat-leaf parsley
1 tablespoon chopped thyme
1 teaspoon kosher salt
½ teaspoon freshly milled black pepper

1. Warm a sauté pan on medium heat for 3 minutes. Add the grape-seed oil, followed by the onion and garlic. Cook the vegetables until tender but not brown, approximately 4 minutes, lowering the heat if necessary.
2. Add the mushrooms and cook on high heat until all the vegetables are dry and begin browning, an additional 5 minutes.
3. Add the wine and deglaze the pan. Add chicken stock and simmer until all of the liquid is evaporated and the mixture is again dry, around 5 minutes. Mix in the butter, herbs, salt, and pepper and serve hot.

Variation: For a more flavorful and exciting side dish, use exotic mushrooms such as shiitake (stems removed), chanterelle, or porcini, either by themselves or in combination.

String Beans with Garlic and Almonds

I have recommended serving this dish with Roasted Chicken with Lemon-Sultana Compote and Roasted Peppers (page 111), but it also goes well with many fish and meat recipes. For a nutritious and filling meal, try it with a piece of grilled flank steak or white, flaky fish such as bass or cod.

MAKES 4 SERVINGS

½ cup blanched and sliced almonds
2 cups string beans
2 tablespoons extra-virgin olive oil
4 garlic cloves, sliced thin
2 tablespoons chiffonade flat-leaf parsley
2 tablespoons chopped chives
1 tablespoon almond oil
Kosher salt
Freshly milled white pepper

1. Toast the almonds by placing them on a baking sheet in the oven or toaster oven and cooking at 350°F until golden brown, approximately 10 minutes. Allow them to cool down before handling.
2. Blanch the string beans in a large pot of boiling salted water for 3 minutes, then drain them in a colander. (The string beans should still be slightly crunchy when they are taken out of the water.)
3. Heat a sauté pan on medium for 3 minutes and then add the olive oil and garlic. Add the string beans and toss, followed by the toasted almonds, parsley, chives, almond oil, and salt and pepper to taste. Serve immediately to maintain the crispness of the string beans.

Variation: Blanched and sliced almonds are readily available at supermarkets; but if you wish to omit the extra step of toasting the almonds, roasted whole almonds (which are also very easy to find) may be used instead.

Sautéed Bean Medley

Fresh beans, including haricots verts, yellow wax beans, and Chinese long beans, are extremely beneficial to a diabetic diet: they are very low in calories and high in fiber, vitamins, and minerals.

MAKES 4 SERVINGS

1 cup haricots verts or green beans
1 cup yellow wax beans
1 cup Chinese long beans (see note) or green beans
2 tablespoons canola oil
1 garlic clove, chopped
1 tablespoon chopped shallots
1 teaspoon chopped ginger
Kosher salt
Freshly milled black pepper

1. Blanch and shock the beans separately in a large pot of salted boiling water. All three beans take a different amount of time to cook, but start checking each after about 2 minutes. (To test for doneness, remove one of the beans from the boiling water and taste—it should still be slightly crunchy.)
2. Heat a sauté pan on medium for 4 minutes and add the canola oil. Add the garlic, shallots, and ginger and mix everything together.
3. After 30 seconds, add the beans, stir, and season with salt and pepper to taste. Sauté until the beans are hot, approximately 3 minutes. Serve the bean medley with fish or poultry.

Note: Chinese long beans are similar in taste and appearance to string beans, but long beans are normally bigger. String beans are fine to use as a substitute in this recipe.

Variation: To serve with meat such as the Pan-Roasted Filet Mignon (page 115), add 1 teaspoon of soy sauce to provide more depth of flavor.

Brussels Sprouts with Mustard Seeds and Curry

For many of us, Brussels sprouts evoke childhood memories of being told to "eat your vegetables, they're good for you." While they are indeed nutritious, Brussels sprouts can also taste wonderful—just be sure not to overcook them, which can produce an unpleasantly strong flavor and smell.

MAKES 4 SERVINGS

2 tablespoons clarified butter (page 15)
1 tablespoon yellow mustard seeds
1 teaspoon Madras curry powder
Kosher salt
2 cups Brussels sprouts
Freshly milled white pepper

1. In a sauté pan, melt the clarified butter and add the mustard seeds and curry. Turn off the heat and allow the ingredients to sit for 10 minutes in the pan.
2. In a large pot, bring 1 gallon of water to a rapid boil. Add 3 table-spoons of salt and return the water to a boil. Add the Brussels sprouts and cook until just tender, approximately 4 minutes, and drain in a colander.
3. Preheat the sauté pan on medium until the butter begins to brown and then add the Brussels sprouts. Toss to coat, allowing the Brussels sprouts to brown lightly. Season with salt and pepper to taste.
4. Serve this side dish with simply grilled flavorful meats, including pork or lamb. Alternatively, Brussels sprouts also pair well with sautéed scallops.

Okra with Slow-Cooked Onions and Spicy Tomato Sauce

Okra is a popular ingredient in the South and is served in many different ways (probably the best-known being gumbo). With a renewed interest in southern cooking throughout the United States, okra has become more popular and easier to find in grocery stores in recent years.

MAKES 8 SERVINGS

1 cup Homemade Tomato Sauce (page 154)
1 tablespoon red pepper flakes
2½ cups okra
Juice of 1 lemon
¼ cup extra-virgin olive oil
4 yellow onions, large dice
4 garlic cloves, sliced
½ cup Gaeta, Kalamata, or Niçoise olives
½ cup flat-leaf parsley, chiffonade
Kosher salt
Freshly milled white pepper

1. Place the tomato sauce and red pepper flakes in a small pot and heat on low until it reaches a simmer. Turn off the heat, cover, and set aside until ready to use.
2. Trim the ends off the okra and immediately place the okra in a bowl filled with cold water and the lemon juice to prevent them from browning.
3. Heat a sauté pan on medium for 3 minutes, add the olive oil and the onions, and stir briefly. Reduce the heat to low and cook the onions until lightly caramelized, stirring often.
4. Add the garlic, olives, okra, and tomato sauce and simmer until the okra becomes tender. Stir in the parsley and season with salt and pepper to taste.

Stewed Ratatouille

Serve the ratatouille on its own as an appetizer, alongside fish, or with poultry dishes such as Slow-Roasted Chicken with Herb Spaetzle and Roasted Mushrooms (page 107).

MAKES 8 SERVINGS

1 cup Homemade Tomato Sauce (page 154)
1 tablespoon red pepper flakes
⅓ cup extra-virgin olive oil
1 onion, large dice
4 garlic cloves, sliced
1 red pepper, julienne
1 yellow pepper, julienne
3 zucchini, sliced
3 yellow squash, sliced
1 small eggplant, quartered and sliced across
½ cup Gaeta, Kalamata, or Niçoise olives
1 bunch flat-leaf parsley, chiffonade
Kosher salt
Freshly milled white pepper

1. Place the tomato sauce and red pepper flakes in a small pot and heat on low to a simmer. Turn off the heat, cover, and set aside until ready to use.
2. Heat a sauté pan on medium and add 1 tablespoon of olive oil. Sauté the onion and garlic together until the onions are translucent, approximately 3 minutes; remove and place in a large bowl.
3. Return the pan to the heat, add 2 tablespoons of olive oil, and sauté the red and yellow peppers for 4 minutes. Remove and add to the bowl with the onions and garlic.
4. Next, sauté the zucchini and yellow squash in 1 tablespoon of olive oil until they begin to lose their firmness, approximately 3 minutes, and add to the bowl.
5. Finally, turn up the heat to medium-high; add 2 more tablespoons of olive oil and sauté the eggplant until it begins to soften, 2 minutes longer. Stir in the tomato sauce, olives, and sautéed vegetables and pour the mixture into a pot.

6. Simmer the vegetables until they are very tender but not mushy, approximately 20 minutes. Add the parsley and season with salt and pepper to taste.

Variation: The method for this recipe calls for sautéing all the vegetables separately to ensure none will overcook, but to save time you can also use the following technique: Pour all the olive oil into a hot pan (use two pans if necessary), followed by the onion and garlic; a minute later, add the peppers, a minute after that the zucchini and yellow squash, and finally the eggplant slices.

Sauté all the vegetables together until they begin to lose their crispness and the onions become translucent, an additional 2 to 3 minutes. Stir in the tomato sauce and olives and proceed with step 6 above.

Sautéed Spinach with Leeks and Feta

Spinach and feta cheese are commonly used together in Greek cooking, and they both pair well with grilled lamb. Alternatively, this side dish will stand up to heartier shrimp entrees, including Grilled Shrimp with Lentil Ragout (page 71).

MAKES 4 SERVINGS

1 bunch leeks, cleaned, small dice
2 tablespoons extra-virgin olive oil
2 garlic cloves, sliced
2 cups spinach leaves, cleaned
Kosher salt
Freshly milled white pepper
¼ cup feta cheese, crumbled
¼ cup fresh lemon juice (from 1 to 2 lemons)

1. Bring a large pot of salted water to a boil. Add the leeks and blanch until tender, approximately 10 to 15 minutes. Drain and set aside until ready to use.
2. Heat a large pan on medium for 3 minutes. Add the olive oil and garlic and sauté briefly. Next, add the spinach and sauté until it begins to wilt, 1 to 2 minutes. Stir in the leeks and season with salt and pepper to taste.
3. Place the spinach mixture on a warm plate, sprinkle the feta cheese and lemon juice on top, and serve hot.

Stuffed Zucchini Blossoms

Until recently, most people in the United States had never heard of zucchini blossoms as an ingredient, even though zucchini is so common here. Zucchini blossoms are still anything but commonplace, however, and they can only be found when in season, from late spring until early fall.

MAKES 4 SERVINGS

1 tablespoon low-fat cream cheese
3 tablespoons soft goat cheese
2 tablespoons grated Romano cheese
1 tablespoon chopped chives
1 tablespoon chopped flat-leaf parsley
1 thyme sprig, picked
Kosher salt
Freshly milled white pepper
12 zucchini blossoms
½ cup flour, sifted
½ cup cornstarch
¼ cup extra-virgin olive oil
¾ cup canola oil

1. Combine the cream cheese, goat cheese, and Romano cheese with the chives, parsley, and thyme, and season with salt and pepper to taste.
2. Place the cheese mixture into a pastry bag and squeeze it into the inside of the blossoms. Gently twist the top of the blossoms closed with your fingers to seal.
3. Mix the flour and cornstarch together in a shallow bowl and roll the blossoms in it to coat.
4. Place the oils in a large sauté pan and heat on medium-high for approximately 4 minutes. Pan-fry the blossoms until golden and crisp, approximately 3 minutes per side.
5. Remove the blossoms from the oil and pat them dry on paper towels. Season with salt and pepper to taste. Serve immediately, either on their own as an hors d'oeuvre or appetizer or with any number of chicken, lamb, or pork dishes.

Open-Faced Mushroom "Ravioli"

Thinly sliced portobello mushrooms serve as a substitute for pasta sheets in this recipe, resulting in a dish that is lower in carbohydrates. The goat cheese provides necessary protein, and the cannellini beans are full of soluble fiber.

MAKES 4 SERVINGS

3 portobello mushrooms, cleaned and stems removed
½ cup Coach Farms or other soft goat cheese
2 cups Roasted Mushrooms (page 133)
Kosher salt
Freshly milled black pepper
One 15-ounce can cannellini beans, drained
1 quart Mushroom Stock (page 41)
½ bunch flat-leaf parsley, chiffonade
2 tablespoons white truffle oil

1. Slice the portobello mushrooms across to create 12 slices that are roughly ⅛ inch thick each and set aside.
2. Puree the goat cheese in a blender along with the roasted mushrooms and season with salt and pepper to taste.
3. In a small pot, cook the beans in approximately ¼ cup of mushroom stock until hot, and reserve.
4. In a separate pot, cook the mushroom–goat cheese mixture on medium-low until hot, stirring often to prevent the ingredients from burning, approximately 4 minutes. Add the parsley and adjust seasonings if necessary.
5. Place one slice of portobello mushroom on the bottom of a bowl, and spoon 4 tablespoons of the mushroom–goat cheese mixture on top. Place another mushroom slice over the mixture to form the "ravioli." Spoon the cannellini beans around the ravioli.

6. Bring the remaining mushroom stock to a simmer. Pour it carefully into the bowl and over the mushroom ravioli, covering the ravioli approximately halfway up; this will soften and cook the portobello mushroom slices. Drizzle some truffle oil over the ravioli and into the broth.

Note: This dish makes a great light entree for lunch or dinner. But by cutting the serving size in half, it also works as a side dish to accompany lower-calorie proteins such as grilled chicken breast or sautéed red snapper.

Asparagus Flan and Sautéed Chanterelles

Chanterelle mushrooms are expensive and often hard to find outside of specialty markets. They are worth seeking out during the summer and fall, though, when they are in season and usually a little more affordable. Oyster mushrooms or shiitakes may be used in place of chanterelles in this recipe.

MAKES 6 SERVINGS

3 cups chanterelles (1¼ pounds)
2 tablespoons extra-virgin olive oil
4 tablespoons minced shallots
¼ cup Vegetable Stock (page 40)
20 asparagus spears (1 pound)
Kosher salt
5 large eggs
2 cups skim milk
1 tablespoon canola oil
½ bunch chervil or ½ bunch flat-leaf parsley, picked
Freshly milled black pepper

1. Brush the mushrooms clean of any debris that may be left on the surface (avoid washing the mushrooms, which will cause them to soak up water).
2. Heat a large sauté pan on medium for 3 minutes. Add the olive oil and shallots, followed by the mushrooms. Cook until the mushrooms begin to soften and shrink, approximately 3 to 4 minutes.
3. Deglaze the mushrooms with the vegetable stock and set aside for approximately 5 minutes in the pan to cool and complete the cooking process.
4. For the flan, blanch the asparagus in a large pot of salted boiling water until tender, approximately 4 to 5 minutes. Shock in ice water and cut into 1-inch pieces.
5. Place half the asparagus in a blender with the eggs and skim milk and puree until smooth.
6. Preheat an oven to 350°F. Pour the flan mixture into six 3-inch ramekins that have been brushed lightly with canola oil and cook them uncovered in a water bath (see note) in the oven for approxi-

mately 25 to 30 minutes. (To check for doneness, place a skewer into the flan—if it comes out clean, the ramekins are ready to be removed from the oven.)

7. Sauté the asparagus and mushrooms together until warm, stir in the chervil, and season with salt and pepper to taste.

8. To serve, place the flan in the center of a plate and surround it with the sautéed mushrooms and asparagus. Serve as an appetizer, or alongside chicken, scallops, veal, or duck for a heartier entree.

Note: A water bath ensures that the flan will cook evenly throughout. To make one, fill a large pot approximately a quarter of the way with warm water; when adding the ramekins, the water should reach approximately halfway up the sides. Be careful not to tip the ramekins over when adding them to the pot!

Variation: For a lighter side dish, simply omit the asparagus flan and serve the asparagus and mushrooms together with fish, poultry, or meat.

Grilled Eggplant Rollatini

Eggplant tends to soak up a lot of oil when it is prepared using such typical methods as pan-frying and sautéing, but by grilling the eggplant for this dish, the amount of oil can be cut way back without sacrificing any flavor.

MAKES 4 APPETIZER SERVINGS

2 tablespoons low-fat cream cheese
3 tablespoons low-fat ricotta
2 tablespoons grated Romano cheese
1 large egg
1 thyme sprig, picked
1 tablespoon chopped chives
1 tablespoon chopped flat-leaf parsley
Kosher salt
Freshly milled white pepper
2 tablespoons extra-virgin olive oil
8 eggplant slices, ¼ inch thick (see note)
2 tablespoons fresh lemon juice

1. Combine the cream cheese, ricotta, and Romano cheese together with the egg, thyme, chives, and parsley, and season with salt and pepper to taste.
2. Heat a grill pan on medium-high, brush with olive oil, and grill the eggplant slices approximately 3 minutes on each side to soften them and form grill marks. Set the eggplant aside to cool.
3. Place 1 tablespoon of the cheese mixture onto the center of each eggplant slice and roll lengthwise into a cigar shape.
4. Preheat the oven to 350°F. Bake the eggplant rollatini in the oven until the cheese has set and the eggplant is fully cooked, approximately 5 minutes. Sprinkle the eggplant rollatini with the lemon and remaining olive oil and serve hot (two per serving).

Note: If possible, use smaller eggplant, which tend to not have as many seeds and as a result are normally less bitter than large eggplant.

Variation: In place of the lemon juice and olive oil, eggplant rollatini also tastes great served with approximately 1 tablespoon of Homemade Tomato Sauce (page 154) poured over each one.

Tofu and Vegetable Stir-Fry

Stir-frying in a wok or sauté pan is a great way to cook vegetables quickly with a small amount of oil. It also helps retain necessary vitamins and minerals, as well as the freshness of the vegetables.

MAKES 4 SERVINGS

1 tablespoon canola oil
1 tablespoon minced ginger
2 garlic cloves, minced
2 bunches scallions, green parts only, julienne
2 cups snow pea pods
2 cups baby bok choy, sliced
1 cup mung bean sprouts
One 8-ounce can sliced water chestnuts
One 15-ounce package firm tofu, large dice
1 teaspoon sesame seeds
1 teaspoon sesame oil
Kosher salt
Freshly milled white pepper

1. Heat a wok or large sauté pan on medium-high for 5 minutes. Add the canola oil and then the ginger, garlic, and scallions.
2. Add the vegetables at approximately 30-second intervals, beginning with the snow pea pods and followed by the bok choy, mung bean sprouts, and water chestnuts. Add the tofu and cook until the snow pea pods are tender, 3 to 4 minutes total.
3. Add the sesame seeds and sesame oil and season with salt and pepper to taste. Serve immediately to maintain the crispness of the snow pea pods and bok choy.

Note: Tofu is packed with protein, calcium, and iron and is low in fat, making this dish a great vegetarian entree for lunch or dinner. For a larger gathering, it also goes well as a side dish with a number of entrees in this book, including Seared Duck Breast with Pumpkin-Seed Vinaigrette (page 127), and in place of the vegetables accompanying the Slow-Roasted Chicken (page 107).

Herb Spaetzle

What pasta is to Italians, spaetzle is to Germans and Austrians. Spaetzle can actually be easier to prepare than pasta, because it is not necessary to roll out the dough and cut it before cooking.

MAKES 10 SERVINGS

Kosher salt
3 cups all-purpose flour
4 large eggs, lightly beaten
1 cup milk or low-fat milk
½ teaspoon sugar
1 teaspoon ground nutmeg
½ teaspoon baking powder
3 tablespoons unsalted butter
1 tablespoon chopped chervil
1 tablespoon chopped thyme
1 tablespoon chopped tarragon
1 tablespoon chopped flat-leaf parsley
1 tablespoon chopped chives

1. Bring a large pot of water to a boil, add ¼ cup salt, and reduce to a simmer. Set aside a bowl filled with ice water.
2. Sift the flour twice and combine it with the eggs, milk, sugar, nutmeg, baking powder, and 2 teaspoons of salt in a bowl.
3. Use a spatula to force the dough through a colander and directly into the pot of boiling water (if necessary, add some more milk or a little water to the mixture to thin it out). Alternatively, dip a fork or slotted spoon into the dough and wave it vigorously over the water to form the spaetzle.
4. In small batches, simmer the spaetzle in the water until they float, approximately 4 to 5 minutes. Cover the pot and allow the spaetzle to cook until they swell up, another 2 to 3 minutes. Immediately place the spaetzle into the ice water, then drain.

5. Heat a sauté pan on medium; add the butter and then the spaetzle. Cook on one side until they begin to brown, approximately 3 minutes. Toss with the herbs in the pan just before serving.

Note: One or more of the herbs called for in this dish may be omitted if desired, particularly the tarragon, which has a stronger flavor than the others.

Quinoa Pasta Salad

The quinoa penne used in this recipe can be found in many health food stores or online, but other shapes, including quinoa rotelle or even quinoa elbows, can be used instead, or wheat pasta may be substituted.

MAKES 6 SERVINGS

2 beefsteak tomatoes, quartered
¼ cup extra-virgin olive oil
2 tablespoons red wine vinegar
1 teaspoon red pepper flakes
Kosher salt
1 garlic clove
1 pound quinoa penne
1 bunch basil, chiffonade
1 bunch tarragon, picked
1 bunch chervil, picked
1 pinch fennel pollen, optional (see note)
1 onion, small dice
Freshly milled white pepper
¼ pound Parmesan, shaved

1. Preheat the oven to 450°F. Cut out the seeds from the tomato quarters using a paring knife. Sprinkle a little olive oil, red wine vinegar, red pepper flakes, and salt over the tomatoes and roast them on a baking sheet in the oven until they begin to brown, approximately 8 to 10 minutes.
2. Remove the tomatoes from the oven, allow them to cool to room temperature, and peel off the skin. Chop the tomatoes into small pieces and set aside.
3. Heat a small pot of water to boiling and blanch the garlic until it becomes soft, approximately 2 to 3 minutes (this will help tame the garlic's sharp bite).
4. Bring a large pot of salted water to a boil. Add the penne and cook until al dente, approximately 8 to 10 minutes.
5. Drain the pasta in a colander, rinse with cold water to stop the cooking process, and mix with 1 teaspoon of olive oil to prevent the penne from sticking to each other.

6. Combine the pasta with the basil, tarragon, chervil, fennel pollen (if using), onion, blanched garlic, and the remaining olive oil, vinegar, and red pepper, and season with salt and pepper to taste. Refrigerate until ready to use. To serve, top with the roasted tomatoes and Parmesan.

Note: Fennel pollen has been appearing on the menus of top restaurants for some time now, but for home use it is quite expensive and can be difficult to find even in gourmet stores. (The Internet may be your best bet.)

Fettuccini with Asparagus, Morels, and Peas

Vegetables are always an important part of a diabetic diet, but they are especially enjoyable in the springtime, when locally grown produce is available from greenmarkets and grocers. To me, asparagus, morels, and peas are the epitome of spring.

MAKES 6 SERVINGS

Kosher salt
14 thin asparagus stalks
1 pound fettuccini or lentil linguini
2 tablespoons extra-virgin olive oil
3 shallots, diced
2 garlic cloves, diced
15 morels or crimini mushrooms, sliced (see note)
1 cup shelled fresh peas
3 plum tomatoes, quartered
½ bunch flat-leaf parsley, chiffonade
1 tablespoon unsalted butter
Freshly milled white pepper
Parmesan

1. Fill a large pot with approximately 1 gallon of water. Add 1 table-spoon of salt and put on the stove to boil.
2. Blanch and shock the asparagus and drain on a paper towel. Cut the asparagus into 1-inch pieces and set aside.
3. Bring a large pot of salted water to a boil. Add the fettuccini and cook until just al dente, approximately 8 minutes. Drain in a colander and set aside.
4. Heat a sauté pan on medium and pour in the olive oil. Add the shallots and garlic and cook until the shallots are translucent, approximately 3 minutes.
5. Next add the morels and fresh peas and sauté until they begin to soften, another 2 to 3 minutes. Follow that with the tomatoes, blanched asparagus, and fettuccini and cook for 2 minutes longer. Stir in the parsley, butter, and salt and pepper to taste. Serve immediately with freshly grated Parmesan.

Note: If using morels, which are expensive and often hard to find even in season, be sure to wash them well inside and out to remove any dirt.

Variation: This dish can be made all year long; just substitute broccoli when asparagus is out of season, and use frozen peas instead of fresh.

Baked Whole-Wheat Ziti with Homemade Tomato Sauce

The traditional Italian-American baked ziti recipe is lightened up a bit here, with low-fat cream cheese and low-fat ricotta substituting for whole-milk ricotta and mozzarella cheese. This recipe also calls for whole-wheat ziti; if you are diabetic but would rather use regular ziti, it is best to cut the portion in half and serve it with a side of vegetables such as sautéed spinach or broccoli.

MAKES 8 SERVINGS

Homemade Tomato Sauce
Two 28-ounce cans whole peeled plum tomatoes
¼ cup extra-virgin olive oil
1 onion, small dice
4 garlic cloves, sliced
1 bunch basil
Kosher salt
Freshly milled white pepper

Baked Ziti
1 tablespoon low-fat cream cheese
4 tablespoons low-fat ricotta
2 tablespoons grated Romano cheese (see note)
1 large egg
1 thyme sprig, picked
1 tablespoon chopped chives
1 tablespoon chopped flat-leaf parsley
Kosher salt
Freshly milled white pepper
3 tablespoons extra-virgin olive oil
1 pound whole-wheat ziti

1. For the tomato sauce, in a large bowl crush the tomatoes by hand until broken up but still chunky and set aside.
2. Heat a Dutch oven or large stainless steel pot on medium. Add the oil, onion, and garlic and simmer until the onions are translucent but not browned, approximately 4 minutes.

3. Add the crushed tomatoes and their liquid and simmer uncovered for 1 hour, stirring occasionally to prevent the bottom from burning.
4. When the sauce has finished cooking, remove the pot from the heat. (For a more traditional, thicker tomato sauce, use a blender or immersion blender to puree the ingredients.)
5. Stir in the basil leaves and season with salt and pepper to taste. Set the tomato sauce aside until ready to use.
6. For the baked ziti, combine the cream cheese, ricotta, and Romano cheese together with the egg, thyme, chives, and parsley and season with salt and pepper to taste. Refrigerate this mixture until the pasta has finished cooking.
7. To make the pasta, bring 1 gallon of water to a boil in a large pot. Add 1 tablespoon of olive oil and 1 tablespoon of salt to the water. Add the ziti and cook until just al dente, approximately 10 minutes, and then drain in a colander.
8. Combine the pasta with the cheese mixture and season with salt and pepper to taste. Toss in 1 cup of tomato sauce and set aside.
9. Brush a casserole dish with the remaining olive oil. Spoon a little sauce into the bottom of the dish, then add the pasta mixture. Even out the mixture in the casserole and top with 1 cup of tomato sauce.
10. Bake covered in a 350°F oven until heated through, approximately 30 to 40 minutes. Allow the baked ziti to cool for 10 minutes, and serve with additional Romano (if desired).

Variation: Romano cheese is typically sharper and more pungent (and less expensive) than Parmesan, but either one can be used for this recipe, depending on your taste.

Chapter 8

Desserts

It was once thought that consuming even a small amount of sugar was unhealthy—and possibly even dangerous—for those suffering from type 2 diabetes. But today it is considered fine for most diabetics to have some sugar in their diet, as long as the daily amount is kept under control.

Monitoring Blood Sugar Levels

The most important dietary advice that diabetics can follow is to be sure your body's overall blood sugar level is kept under control. In some people, that might mean having to cut most sugary foods out of their diet, but monitoring your glucose levels closely is the only way to know for sure.

In particular, foods high in simple carbohydrates and refined sugars without any real nutritional value do not contribute anything positive to a diabetic diet. Too much of these types of foods, and the result will be weight gain accompanied by numerous health issues such as heart disease, high blood pressure, and even liver failure related to diabetes. Instead, replace these empty calories with foods that contain protein, fiber, and other nutrients. Some simple carbohydrates that diabetics should try to stay away from are regular sodas, candy bars, most breakfast cereals, and fruit preserves.

Fruit: Nature's Sugar

According to the American Diabetes Association, fructose (the natural sugar found in fruits) may have less of an effect on blood glucose levels than table sugar or other carbohydrates. This is because fructose is absorbed by the body more slowly than other types of sugar. So whenever possible, people with diabetes should attempt to cure their sweet tooth by eating fruit rather than consuming refined table sugar or artificial sweeteners.

Fruits also contain a number of different vitamins, as well as dietary fiber, and of course they are low in fat. For example, one medium apple contains about 21 grams of carbohydrates and 5 grams of dietary fiber. One cup of strawberries contains roughly 10 grams of carbohydrates and 84 milligrams of vitamin C—140 percent of the RDA (recommended dietary allowance) for this vitamin. And one-quarter of a whole cantaloupe has about 11 grams of carbohydrates and 40 percent of the RDA of vitamin A. On the other hand, one 12-ounce can of Coca-Cola contains a whopping 41 grams of carbohydrates and has absolutely no recognized nutritional value.

When using fruit as the main ingredient in a dessert, I always make an effort to keep vitamins and other nutrients from leaching out during the cooking process. For example, the recipe for Cuisson of Honeydew Melon with Watermelon Gelée (page 163) requires only a minimal amount of cooking; the resulting dessert is both delicious and good for you, without the addition of any table sugar or artificial sweeteners.

As a chef, I also like to use ingredients in my desserts that many people would not normally consider, such as spices and salt. If properly utilized, these flavorings can accentuate the natural sugars in different fruits, allowing you to cut back on the amount of sugar needed to flavor a dish; for example, the pineapple in my Pink Peppercorn Pineapple recipe (page 165) is seasoned with pepper, curry powder, salt, and balsamic vinegar—you have to taste it to believe it!

Warm Baked Apple with Golden Raisins and Walnuts

Serve these luscious baked apples with a little vanilla frozen yogurt or sugar-free vanilla ice cream for a healthful dessert that tastes downright sinful. Apple pie à la mode, anyone?

MAKES 6 SERVINGS

1 tablespoon ground cinnamon
1 teaspoon ground ginger
1 teaspoon ground nutmeg
2 tablespoons golden raisins
¼ cup chopped walnuts
1 tablespoon honey
2 tablespoons unsalted butter, softened
3 Rome Beauty apples

1. In a bowl, mix the cinnamon, ginger, and nutmeg with the raisins, nuts, and honey. Add approximately 3 tablespoons of water and the butter.

2. Slice the apples in half lengthwise. Core and place the halves in muffin tins with the cut side up. Use tins that are large enough to accommodate the apples comfortably without allowing too much room for expansion.

3. Fill the scooped-out center of each apple half with the raisin-nut mixture. Cover the apples very loosely with aluminum foil and bake in a 300°F oven for 25 minutes.

4. Remove the foil and return the apples to the oven for an additional 10 minutes, until they begin to brown. Allow them to cool slightly before serving.

Note: Apples and other fruit such as pears and avocados will begin to discolor very soon after they are cut and exposed to the air. To prevent this from happening, do not slice the apples until they are ready to be stuffed, and then immediately place them in the oven to cook.

Variation: I like to use sweet, juicy Rome Beauty apples for this recipe because they hold their shape well when baked, but Granny Smith or Macintosh apples will also do quite nicely.

Splenda Panna Cotta

Splenda is a great sugar substitute for diabetics, because it contains very few carbohydrates and calories (1 cup of Splenda has 96 calories and 24 grams of carbohydrate, compared with 770 calories and 192 grams of carbohydrate for 1 cup of sugar). Try it for yourself and see if you can tell the difference.

MAKES 6 SERVINGS

4 cups skim milk
½ cup Splenda
5 sheets gelatin or 1 tablespoon plus ½ teaspoon powdered
   gelatin, bloomed (see Gelatin on page 17)
1 ruby red grapefruit, sectioned

1. Warm the skim milk and Splenda in a small pot. Add the bloomed gelatin sheets and stir until dissolved. Pour into six 3-inch ramekins and allow the panna cotta to set in the refrigerator for 3 to 4 hours.
2. Top with the grapefruit sections and serve.

Variation: Instead of grapefruit, the panna cotta can be topped with chopped strawberries or other ripe fruit.

Strawberry Panna Cotta

Panna cotta is a great dessert to serve at a dinner party if you want to impress your friends without overburdening yourself—it is simple to prepare and can be made up to 2 days in advance, so all you have to do is remove it from the refrigerator and garnish before serving.

MAKES 4 SERVINGS

1 pint strawberries, hulled
2 tablespoons fresh lemon juice
2 tablespoons fresh orange juice
1 pint skim milk
1 tablespoon thyme leaves
1 teaspoon kosher salt
4 tablespoons Splenda
2 sheets gelatin or ½ tablespoon powdered gelatin, bloomed (see Gelatin on page 17)

1. Place half of the strawberries in a small saucepot and heat together with the lemon juice and orange juice. Bring the ingredients to a simmer and cook until the strawberries lose their shape, approximately 5 minutes.
2. In a separate pot, heat the skim milk and thyme just to a boil. Remove the pot from the heat and allow the ingredients to steep for 5 minutes. Strain out the thyme leaves and place the milk in the refrigerator to cool.
3. Puree the milk with the cooked strawberries, salt, and Splenda and add the bloomed gelatin. Allow the mixture to cool slightly and pour into four 3-inch ramekins.
4. Place the ramekins in the refrigerator to set for 3 hours. Meanwhile, slice the remaining strawberries and set aside. Serve the panna cotta still in its ramekin, garnished with the strawberry slices.

Blueberry Panna Cotta

Traditional Italian panna cotta is made with cream or milk, but I find that by using skim milk and gelatin, it is possible to reproduce the same luscious mouth feel without all the calories (which is why I have included three different recipes for panna cotta in this chapter).

MAKES 4 SERVINGS

1 pint blueberries
2 tablespoons fresh lemon juice
2 tablespoons fresh orange juice
1 pint skim milk
1 tablespoon chopped basil
1 teaspoon kosher salt
4 tablespoons Splenda
2 sheets gelatin or ½ tablespoon powdered gelatin, bloomed (see Gelatin on page 17)

1. Place half of the blueberries in a small saucepot and heat together with the lemon juice and orange juice. Bring the ingredients to a simmer and cook until the blueberries lose their shape, approximately 5 minutes.
2. In a separate pot, heat the skim milk and basil just to a boil. Remove the pot from the heat and allow the ingredients to steep for 5 minutes. Strain out the basil leaves and place the milk in the refrigerator to cool.
3. Puree the milk with the cooked blueberries, salt, and Splenda, and add the bloomed gelatin. Allow the mixture to cool slightly and pour into four 3-inch ramekins.
4. Place the ramekins into the refrigerator and allow the panna cotta to set for 3 hours. (The panna cotta can also be made up to 2 days in advance and refrigerated until ready to use.) Serve the panna cotta still in its ramekin, garnished with the remaining fresh blueberries.

Variation: To mix things up a bit at your next dinner party, make both this panna cotta and the Strawberry Panna Cotta (page 161); serve the Blueberry Panna Cotta to some guests and the Strawberry Panna Cotta to others.

Cuisson of Honeydew Melon with Watermelon Gelée

Using gelatin may seem a bit intimidating to some, but gelatin sheets (or the more common gelatin powder) are actually very easy to use as long as the correct proportion is maintained—just think of it as fancy Jell-O.

MAKES 6 SERVINGS

1 ripe honeydew melon
2 tablespoons fresh lemon juice
2 teaspoons kosher salt
1 seedless watermelon (approximately 5 pounds)
2 tablespoons fresh lime juice
12 gelatin sheets or 3 tablespoons gelatin powder, bloomed (see Gelatin on page 17)

1. For the cuisson (broth), cut open the honeydew, discard the seeds, and scoop out the flesh. Puree the melon and lemon juice in a blender until smooth. Strain the puree through a fine mesh strainer lined with cheesecloth, season with 1 teaspoon of salt, and refrigerate for a minimum of 1½ hours.
2. Scoop out the watermelon flesh and puree in a blender with the lime juice. Strain through a fine mesh strainer and season with the remaining salt.
3. Heat the watermelon juice until warm and stir in the gelatin to dissolve. Pour the mixture into a 9-inch-square nonstick cake pan and chill in the refrigerator until set, approximately 1½ hours.
4. To serve, pour some of the honeydew broth into a bowl. Cut the watermelon gelée into 1-inch squares and place into the center of the bowl for a beautiful contrast of color, flavor, and texture.

Mango and Avocado Carpaccio with Pineapple Yogurt Glace

Avocado may not normally seem like a good match for either mango or pineapple, but in this refreshing tropical dish the avocado is used more to provide texture and color rather than for its flavor.

MAKES 4 SERVINGS

Pineapple Yogurt Glace
1 large pineapple
¼ cup Splenda
2 cups nonfat yogurt

Mango and Avocado Carpaccio
1 passion fruit, peeled
¼ cup mint leaves, chiffonade
2 mangoes
2 Hass avocados

1. For the glace, first peel and core the pineapple, then puree the flesh in a blender.
2. Combine the pineapple puree with the Splenda, yogurt, and ½ cup of cold water and freeze using an ice cream maker.
3. For the carpaccio, combine the passion fruit flesh with 1 cup of cold water in a blender and puree until smooth. Strain through a fine mesh strainer and stir in the mint chiffonade.
4. Slice the mango and avocado as thinly as possible. Place a third of the mango on the bottom of a bowl, followed by half the avocado, another third of the mango, the remaining avocado, and a final layer of mango on top.
5. Pour the passion fruit broth over the mango and avocado carpaccio. Place a small scoop of the glace on top of the carpaccio and garnish with a mint leaf.

Variation: If you do not own an ice cream maker or just don't feel like using one, Edy's now makes a line of sugar-free ice cream that is available in many supermarkets.

Pink Peppercorn Pineapple and Vanilla Syrup

Most people would not think of using spices such as peppercorns and curry powder when making dessert, but mixing savory and sweet ingredients is considered perfectly normal in Indian cooking.

MAKES 6 TO 8 SERVINGS

1 vanilla bean
1 cup sugar
1 very ripe pineapple, diced, chilled
3 tablespoons pink peppercorns, crushed (see note)
3 tablespoons extra-virgin olive oil
1 tablespoon Madras curry powder
Hawaiian red sea salt (or any coarse sea salt)
Freshly milled black pepper
25-year-old balsamic vinegar, optional
Micro greens, optional

1. For the vanilla syrup, split the vanilla bean in half lengthwise and place in a saucepot with the sugar and 1 cup of water. Bring to a boil, stirring as you go to dissolve the sugar.
2. Simmer and stir often until the mixture reduces and becomes thicker, approximately 5 minutes. Cool the syrup before removing the vanilla bean and store tightly covered in the refrigerator for up to 2 months.
3. Toss the cold diced pineapple with the peppercorns, olive oil, 1 tablespoon of vanilla syrup, curry powder, and salt and pepper to taste, and place in the refrigerator to macerate for 20 minutes.
4. To serve, lay out the pineapple pieces and drizzle the balsamic vinegar (if using) lightly around but not on top of the pineapple. Sprinkle with the micro greens to garnish, if using.

Note: Pink peppercorns are sweeter than black and white peppercorns, and their attractive color goes well with the yellow of the pineapple.

Variation: In place of micro greens as a garnish, you can use a mix of basil and mint chiffonade.(Micro greens are the tiny leaves and stems of newly sprouting vegetables such as broccoli, arugula and watercress.)

Appendix

Website Resources

American Diabetes Association
www.diabetes.org

Canadian Diabetes Association
www.diabetes.ca

Centers for Disease Control and Prevention
www.cdc.gov/diabetes/

Diabetes UK
www.diabetes.org.uk

Juvenile Diabetes Research Foundation International
www.jdrf.org

MedlinePlus
www.nlm.nih.gov/medlineplus/diabetes.html

National Institutes of Health
www.ndep.nih.gov/

National Diabetes Information Clearinghouse
www.diabetes.niddk.nih.gov/

Books

American Diabetes Association Complete Guide to Diabetes
The American Diabetes Association

Betty Crocker's Diabetes Cookbook: Everyday Meals, Easy as 1-2-3
Betty Crocker Editors

Diabetes for Dummies
Alan L. Rubin

Dr. Bernstein's Diabetes Solution: The Complete Guide to Achieving Normal Blood Sugars
Richard K. Bernstein

Mastering Your Diabetes
Janette Kirkham, RN, CDE, EMT

The Diabetes Food and Nutrition Bible
Hope S. Warshaw, Robyn Webb

The First Year—Type 2 Diabetes: An Essential Guide for the Newly Diagnosed
Gretchen Becker

What to Do When You Have Type 2 Diabetes
The American Diabetes Association

Index

Ace-K, xxv
acesulfame potassium, xxv
Agriculture Department, U.S., 98
alcohol, xxii
All-Clad cookwear, 14
almond(s):
    -cauliflower puree, 61
    goat cheese, on a caraway tuile,
        mâche with, 31–32
    string beans with garlic and, 134
American Diabetes Association, xvi, 66,
    158
Annals of Internal Medicine, xx
antipasto, marinated mushroom, 132
apple:
    -avocado napoleon, seared lamb
        loin with, 123–24
    warm baked, with golden raisins
        and walnuts, 159
artichoke oreganata puree, 62–63
artificial sweeteners, xxv–xxvi
arugula:
    and mizuna salad, 28

    with walnuts, blue cheese, and
        Asian pears, 29
Asian pears, arugula with walnuts, blue
    cheese, and Asian pears, 29
Asian vegetables, poached filet mignon
    with egg noodles and, 117–18
asparagus:
    fettuccini with morels, peas and,
        152–53
    flan and sautéed chanterelles,
        144–45
aspartame, xxv
avocado:
    -apple napoleon, seared lamb loin
        with, 123–24
    carpaccio, and mango with
        pineapple yogurt glace, 164
    -tomatillo salsa, chicken paillard
        with quinoa pilaf and, 105–6

baked whole-wheat ziti with homemade
    tomato sauce, 154–55

flank steak with Chinese vegetables, 121–22

fluke tartare and cucumber-radish salad, 82

foam, pea, grilled scallops with, 77

fond, 10

Food and Drug Administration, U.S., xxvi

fragrant spice-rubbed roast pork loin, 113–14

fresh herbs, 16

fruit(s), xix
    in desserts, 158, 159–65
    sugar in, xix, 158
    see also specific fruits

garlic, string beans with almonds and, 134

gelatin, 17

gelée, watermelon, cuisson of honeydew melon with, 163

ghee, 16

ginger:
    -carrot puree, 59
    -lemon vinaigrette, three-bean salad with, 33–34

glace, mango and avocado carpaccio with pineapple yogurt, 164

glycemic index (GI), xiv–xv

goat cheese:
    almond, on a caraway tuile, mâche with, 31–32
    torta, lamb, beet and, 125–26

grains, 129, 148–55
    complex, 130–31
    see also specific grains

grandma's chicken soup, 51–52

grapeseed oil, 17–18

Greek salad:
    chicken souvlaki with cucumber-yogurt sauce and, 103–4
    modern, 25

grilled:
    bronzino with burst tomatoes and basil-cumin pesto, 93–94
    calamari with cucumber-tomato salad, 73–74
    eggplant rollatini, 146

halibut and buckwheat salad, 89

lamb tenderloin salad, 36

salmon with slow-cooked fennel and cucumber-yogurt sauce, 83–84

scallops with pea foam, 77

shrimp with lentil ragout, 71–72

shrimp with shaved fennel, 69–70

grill pans, 13

halibut:
    grilled, and buckwheat salad, 89
    olive-oil-poached, with braised fennel, 90–91

herb(s):
    fresh, 16
    spaetzle, 148–49
    spaetzle, slow-roasted chicken with roasted mushrooms and, 107–8

herbes de Provence, roasted chicken with, 109–10

homemade tomato sauce, baked whole-wheat ziti with, 154–55

honeydew melon, cuisson of, with watermelon gelée, 163

hydrogenated fats, *see* trans fats

ingredients, basic, 15–19

insulin, xi–xii, xiv, xx

Italian bread croutons, Caesar salad with, 26–27

Japanese stock (dashi), 46

jicama, beef carpaccio with cucumber, watermelon and, 100

Journal of the American Medical Association, xx

juicing, 11

julienne, 11

knives, 12–13
    cuts using, 11–12
    sharpening of, 12

kosher salt, 17

About the Author

FRANKLIN BECKER, a graduate of the Culinary Institute of America and himself a type 2 diabetic, has worked as an executive chef at several of New York City's premier restaurants, including Trinity, Capitale, Cucina, and Local. He was also private chef for Revlon magnate Ron Perelman. Becker's "New American" style of cooking has been praised by *The New York Times* and *New York* magazine. He lives in New York City.

About the Type

The text of this book was set in Berkeley, a variation of the University of California Old Style, which was created by Frederick Goudy. While capturing the feel and traits of its predecessor, Berkeley shows influences from Kennerly, Goudy Old Style, Deepdene, and Booklet Oldstyle, all of which were also designed by Goudy. It is characterized by its calligraphic weight stress, and its generous ascenders and descenders provide variation in text color and easy legibility.